OUTDOOR LIFE

THE ULTIMATE SURVIVAL COOKBOOK

OUTDOOR LIFE

THE ULTIMATE SURVIVAL COOKBOOK

TIM MACWELCH
AND THE EDITORS OF
OUTDOOR LIFE

weldon**owen**

SURVIVAL PRIORITIES

OUTDOOR LIFE

THE ULTIMATE SURVIVAL COOKBOOK

TIM MACWELCH
AND THE EDITORS OF
OUTDOOR LIFE

weldon**owen**

SURVIVAL PRIORITIES

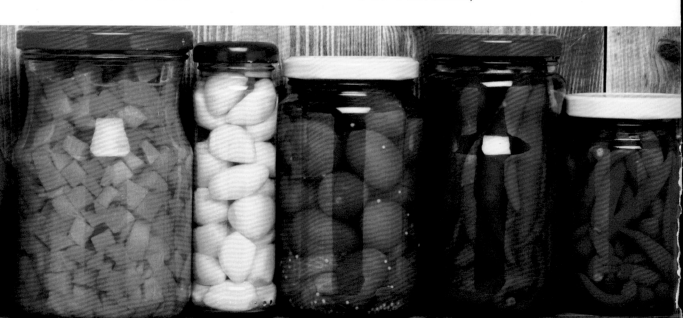

PLANT & ANIMAL FOODS

EATING AFTER A CRISIS

THE FIRST COOKS

With a topic like "cooking as a survival skill," it's only right that we begin the book with the most humble origins and the people who first benefited from the complex interaction between heat and food. Let's go back to (what I imagine as) the first time something edible was "cooked" in the vicinity of humans. Was it curiosity, bravery, or hunger that inspired our remote ancestors to explore the aftermath of a primordial grassland wildfire?

I can almost see our simple predecessors, picking through the blowing ash and blackened char of the fire-swept landscape, and finding an abundance of crispy little roasted animals (most of these unfortunate creatures being charred beyond recognition and nutrition). Yet with enough prowling, these hungry hominids would have eventually found the smoking remains of a larger carcass—an animal killed by the fire, but too large to be devoured by it. That first taste of rare roast beast must have been a good bite, as it inspired our forebears to capture that scary orange thing we call "fire," confine it in a hearth, and use it on a regular basis to transform all kinds of food resources.

And from these rudimentary origins, our path was forever altered. The acts of boiling liquids and cooking foods made them safe to consume, and in many cases the foods were even transformed into a more digestible substance. At the risk of overselling it, I believe that cooking helped our fragile species to survive in the hostile landscape of prehistory. And even though our technologies have advanced from the Stone Age to the Space Age, the importance of cooking hasn't changed after countless centuries. We still need to use our age-old cooking skills to survive in tough times and emergency settings, just as our ancestors did. And who knows—you might even be a great survival cook! Let's find out.

DISASTER
PREPAREDNESS

Preparing a meal from "survival food" doesn't have to mean opening another crate of MREs (military rations) or cracking open your 200th tin of sardines. We all need to eat, especially when we're in dire straits. Those calories are the fuel that will help us get out of that situation.

Yet this doesn't have to mean forcing down survival rations (not all of the time, anyway). This book is your pathway to eating well in tough times, and even during easier times. Our goal is to expand your perspective on the concept of eating to live—as well as living to eat. In this first chapter, we'll take a look at the foundations of preparedness, as they relate to food storage and cooking during natural disasters and other emergencies. Ask anyone who went grocery shopping in the early days of the 2020 pandemic, and they'll tell you what it feels like to experience food insecurity. Bare shelves in your local grocery store, and bare shelves in your pantry at home, can leave a person in a precarious situation. This food shortage (not to mention the toilet paper shortage) should have taught us all some valuable lessons, inspiring us to prepare ourselves and our loved ones before the next disaster hits. If you're still reading, I'll bet you paid attention to these food instability issues, and you never want to feel that helpless again. Well, you're in luck. This first chapter will focus on food storage as a foundation for disaster survival, and we'll even give you the tools and techniques to make (most of) that food taste good.

001 SET YOUR SURVIVAL PRIORITIES

If the worst happens and you need to survive until you're found or can find your way out, you need to prioritize–and fast. Here's what you should concentrate on, in order, starting with your most immediate need and moving toward less-pressing issues.

SHELTER This is always your top survival priority (unless there is a dire medical issue). Your shelter will need to protect you from the cold or the heat, depending on the scenario. Build a thick, insulated shelter for cold conditions. Construct a shady, open one in hot, sunny climates. Remember that your clothes are a form of shelter, too. Stuff them with insulation if you're getting too cold.

WATER You can only make it a few days without water. Boil or treat your water for safety if you can. When faced with the choice between drinking questionable water or dying due to dehydration, drink the water. It's better to be sick and alive than pathogen-free and dead.

FIRE AND SIGNALING Fire is an outstanding distress signal. It also boils your water, cooks your food, and gives you light and heat. Carry multiple fire-starting methods to ensure your success, no matter the weather conditions.

FOOD While the average person could survive a month without eating, there's usually no need for that kind of suffering. Follow the tips, tricks, and information in this book, and you'll have the food priority covered.

How you store your food has a great bearing on its longevity. Anyone storing more than a week's worth of food in his or her home should consider these points:

KEEP COOL (AND DRY) Find a cool place to prevent food loss from heat. A dry basement is ideal, but a closet can also work. Metal cans with food-safe desiccant packs are a great way to save food from moisture, light, insects, and rodents. Food-grade buckets are pretty handy, and oxygen-absorbing packets can also extend the life of stored food.

LIGHTS OFF This part is easy; most containers are lightproof. But if you do end up with a stock of food in clear jars or plastic containers, keep the storage area dark to prevent light from reacting with the food.

BUG OUT Rodents and bugs can play havoc in your food. Metal canisters or glass jars can keep them out.

KEEP TIME Depending on the food item and type, it could be nitrogen-packed, freeze-dried, or in a vacuum-sealed package for best shelf life. Otherwise, go with canned food and rotate your stock often. Put the new cans in the back, and use the older cans first.

BE CREATIVE Stash your goods in basements, closets, or garages, or create storage spaces under furniture.

FREEZE SMART Dry goods can stay frozen indefinitely, but not wet-packed foods. Avoid breaking or exploding containers by keeping your stuff from freezing.

BE STRONG Make sure any shelving is sturdy; your jars of food won't help anybody when they have smashed everywhere due to a flimsy shelf or a cheap, collapsed bookcase. Don't keep your food where it can be easily stolen. And in earthquake-prone areas, keep the food in bins on the ground.

003 PACK IT IN PETE

For long-term storage of dry goods, consider using bottles made of PETE (polyethylene terephthalate) plastic (abbreviated PET). Many standard bottles are made of PET (look under the recycling symbol), but you should buy new–not reuse old food or drink packaging. A lot of plastic is too flimsy or porous to block moisture, oxygen, and pests. But PET, when used in combination with oxygen-absorbing packets, does the job. Only use this kind of packaging for dry foods; moist foods must be handled more carefully to avoid the danger of botulism (see item 033). Bottles should be no bigger than 1 gallon (4 liters) for optimal effectiveness.

STEP 1 Test the bottle's seal by closing it tightly, placing under water, and pressing on the lid or cap. If bubbles escape, the seal is faulty and should not be used.

STEP 2 Place an oxygen absorber (a packet of iron powder that helps keep food fresh) in the bottle.

STEP 3 Fill your bottle with dry goods (wheat, corn, dry beans, etc.).

STEP 4 Wipe the bottle's top sealing edge clean with a dry cloth, and screw on the lid tightly.

STEP 5 Store the sealed bottle in a cool, dry location away from direct light. If you use a bottle's contents, add a new oxygen absorber when you refill it.

004 START WITH THE BASICS

It's debatable what's absolutely essential for your survival pantry and what's "nice to have." Here are staples you should at least consider.

SALT It makes your food taste better, helps you preserve meats, and lasts pretty much forever. Almost all salt sold commercially is iodized–but check to be sure. You need the iodine for thyroid health.

BAKING POWDER This pantry essential is used in cooking, but it's also good for cleaning, deodorizing, other household chores.

FATS AND OILS Vegetable shortening has fairly long shelf life. Olive oil is healthy but tends to go bad quicker, so buy it in smaller bottles. Coconut oil is a favorite (see item 029).

SUGAR AND OTHER SWEETS White sugar can be stored for a long period if packaged right (see item 015). Honey and molasses are good to have on hand for cooking.

RICE Rice is a go-to staple that has kept large portions of this planet's population alive. Combine with beans to boost nutrients.

BEANS Sure, beans and rice are practically a prepper cliché, but dried beans can last for up to 30 years and are full of nutrients.

VITAMINS No matter how well your pantry is stocked, you may not get the variety that would be ideal in your diet. Supplement with a multipurpose vitamin and mineral pill just to be sure.

CANNED GOODS Stock up on a good selection of fruits and vegetables–be sure to get a variety for extra nutrition and to prevent boredom if you're eating out of your stockpiles for a while.

COFFEE AND TEA Some people might class these beverages under luxuries, not essentials, but even if you're not a giant fan of coffee, it can be a fantastic trade good, so you should stock at least a few cans.

DRIED FRUIT A great way to store fruit for the long term and a fantastic source of concentrated nutrition. A handful of raisins can sweeten your morning cereal, and dried apricots make a portable source of energy. Buy in bulk or make your own (see item 162).

005 POWER UP WITH PROTEIN

Protein is absolutely essential to your everyday health, and most of us already eat less than we should–even without the additional stress of trying to survive heavy weather or other challenges. Here are some key protein sources to keep on hand.

HARD CHEESE In Europe, people stash cheeses for months or even years inside cool, dark caves. The secret? A good coating of wax. It's not easy to find hard, waxed cheeses in the United States, but they are available, and the little search to find a wax-clad wheel of Parmesan will be worth it in 10 years when you grate it on your postapocalyptic pasta.

JERKY Dried meat or fish is close to 100 percent protein, and it lasts a long, long time (Native Americans and other cultures made jerky for long-term use and easy transport). Buy all-natural products that have fewer additives–the same stuff that keeps it "moist" also makes it spoil more quickly. You can also make your own (see item 116).

CANNED AND DRIED FISH Stock your pantry with canned tuna and salmon, as well as surprisingly versatile sardines (see item 109). All fish are a great source of omega-3 fatty acids, and any fish that has tiny, edible bones, such as kippers, also provides a good dose of calcium.

WHEY PROTEIN Protein powder isn't just for gym rats! It has a long shelf life and a high protein content–a small scoop can have as much protein as a whole steak. Stir into water or milk for a high-protein, on-the-go meal replacement.

NUTS AND NUT BUTTERS Nuts can go bad relatively quickly, but they're a good source of protein, healthy fats, and calories, so it makes sense to have some on hand. Buy peanut butter in smaller jars so you only have to open and use as needed.

DEHYDRATED MILK It's nutritious and long-lasting when nitrogen-packaged, and can be used in cooking or to add to that coffee you hoarded. You did remember to hoard the coffee, didn't you?

006 GO CARB CRAZY

The modern fear of carbs is just that: modern. For most of history, humans have relied on starchy foods for energy, comfort, and nutrients.

WHOLE-WHEAT FLOUR Whole-grain flour does spoil more quickly than the white stuff, but it also has a lot more nutrients. Store it carefully.

DRIED CORN This Native American staple has a very long shelf life and can be ground up to make grits, polenta, and cornbread. Or if you want to get really old-school, look into making masa harina (or just buy some premade for your pantry). This corn flour processed with lime is used to make nutritious corn tortillas.

OATMEAL Buy whole steel-cut oats, and you have a versatile staple that can be cooked up for breakfast or used in baking to add nutrients and fiber.

CRACKERS You don't get a lot of nutrition from crackers, but they have a long shelf life, are easy to eat, and can be a good snack for kids (or grown-ups!) who need some sense of normalcy in a tough situation. Never underestimate the calming power of peanut butter and saltines!

PASTA AND NOODLES Dried pasta lasts virtually forever and, if you buy the fortified kind, can be a source of some vitamins as well. Ramen noodles aren't terribly good for you, but they're easy to cook and can be a nice comfort food.

007 HAVE A STORAGE PLAN

Unless you know for sure that the apocalypse is tomorrow, don't come home with a van-load of random foods on your first trip to the store. Most people don't bother to think beyond the very short term when it comes to meals, but with a little planning and a few calculations, you can develop a short- to medium-term plan for food storage and survival meal planning (and expand it to several months' worth of food). Whether you decide to stuff your kitchen pantry to the ceiling or turn an entire room into a food storage locker, you should start off slowly and deliberately. Stocking up on supplies (especially food) should be done thoughtfully and carefully. In addition to storing shelf-stable, ready-to-eat foods (like snacks), you'll also want to build a canned-goods stockpile and even some long-term food storage. Buy samples of each food item you are considering, and incorporate them into regular meals to test their flavor, texture, and digestibility. Stock up on foods that are long-lasting, easy to prepare, and a hit with your eaters. Generally speaking, you get what you pay for in food-storage products, but even some of the expensive items may not sit well in your family's collective stomach. What good is a bucket or barrel or pallet of freeze-dried beet roots if they taste terrible or create a line for the bathroom? Build a menu and test it before you make an investment.

008 ROTATE SUPPLIES

Rotating your stock is all about timing! You want to eat up your aging food and replace it with fresher products while allowing plenty of buffer time–you don't want your oldest items to expire the day after the emergency begins. These tips will get you going in the right direction.

STEP 1 Plan for success while you're still standing in the store. Look at comparable products, or the boxes at the back of the shelf, to find the longest shelf life or most distant expiration date.

STEP 2 Once you get home, use a permanent marker to write the expiration date in bigger script on the bottle, can, or jar you bought. This saves time later when you're inspecting your supplies.

STEP 3 Place the new item in the back of the pantry, ideally behind another of the same item. If you always add to the front, sooner or later, you'll have a dusty old can of beans in the back that expired ten years ago. So always add to the back and use from the front.

STEP 4 Pick a date. Write a note on your calendar to inspect your food storage every season. This helps you to spot any trouble (like pests) and catch aging items. Many products can be safely used past their expiration date, but it's best if you don't have to eat old food.

009 FEED WITH FIFO

A basic rule of any food pantry is "First In, First Out." What that means: Keep track of the expiration dates on items, and swap them out as they approach culinary old age. That bagged rice is good for a year? After 11 months, replace it with a new bag and enjoy a nice jambalaya. You should never have to throw anything away–just keep using ingredients and replacing them as needed. That way, if and when disaster does strike, dinner's not going to be expired okra served over bug-infested rice.

010 STASH SOME TREATS

Man (and woman and especially child) doth not live by whey powder and canned tomatoes alone. If you're going to be eating from your pantry for more than a few days, you want to be sure it will provide variety and enjoyment as well as sheer nutrition. Even Soylent Green tastes better with a little horseradish.

HERBS AND SPICES A dash of hot sauce or a sprinkling of oregano can make a bland survival dish into a real meal. Grow fresh herbs and chile peppers in your kitchen garden (see item 48), and stock your pantry with some versatile basics. Tabasco and soy sauces last virtually forever, cinnamon and ginger spice up desserts and tea, and spice blends (Italian seasoning, Chinese five-spice, etc.) make cooking easy.

CONDIMENTS Most condiments spoil pretty quickly, so buy them in smaller bottles and open as needed. Flavored vinegars have a very long shelf life and can liven up all kinds of dishes.

SWEETS Bags of chocolate chips and bars of high-quality chocolate last well if stored in a cool place. Cocoa powder and chocolate syrup are also good treats in tough times.

PERSONAL FAVORITES While making your bulk purchases of those essential canned tomatoes, corn, beans, and peaches, throw in some quirky indulgences that will brighten your day even if the power's out and the water's rising. That might be fancy stuffed olives in a jar, hearts of palm, pumpkin pie filling, or whatever else might lift your spirits after a week or two of oatmeal and bean soup.

011 SPICE THINGS UP

It's been said that variety is the spice of life, but I would argue that spice is the spice of life. Since the staples of food storage tend to be bland, spices and seasonings can add some much needed dimension to your dishes and ward off palate fatigue (the feeling of revulsion from eating the exact same thing too many times). Let's change the assumption that "survival food" is just tasteless caloric input. Individual spices and seasonings can work wonders for you, but you can take it to the next level by assembling your own seasoning blends using a handful of different spices, herbs, and other ingredients.

BBQ RUB This spice mix is a great rub for meat, prior to cooking. It's also useful when trying to add that barbecue flavor to side dishes and snacks.

MEXICAN Full of warm, rich flavors, a good Mexican spice blend can turn any ground meat into taco and burrito filling. It's also a surprise ingredient in soups and stews.

ITALIAN Loaded with some of the most quintessential flavors of the northern Mediterranean, an Italian seasoning blend can transform many savory foods.

CHILI BLEND This blend combines the flavors of the American Southwest, making the perfect seasoning for a big pot of chili con carne or chili cheese dip.

STEAK SEASONING The sizzle alone won't sell that steak, but a fine steak seasoning blend can take that boring slab of meat to the next level.

SEASONING SALT This seasoning mix is the most versatile of them all. Apply your homemade seasoning salt to virtually any savory dish for your own "house" spice blend.

BBQ RUB

In a small bowl stir together 1 cup (200 g) brown sugar, 2 tablespoons (10 g) each paprika, smoked paprika, black pepper, salt, chili powder, mustard powder, garlic powder, onion powder, and 2 teaspoons (3 g) cayenne pepper (optional). Store in a glass jar with a lid in a cool, dry place. Makes about 2 cups (305 g).

STEAK SEASONING

In a small bowl stir together ½ cup (150 g) kosher salt, ½ cup (120 g) ground black pepper, ½ cup (90 g) garlic powder, ¼ cup (30 g) paprika, ¼ cup (30 g) onion powder, 2 tablespoons (10 g) dried rosemary, 1 tablespoon (5 g) dried thyme, and 1 tablespoon (5 g) ground coriander. Store in a glass jar with a lid in a cool, dry place. Makes about 2 cups (440 g).

SEASONED SALT

In a small bowl stir together 1 cup (290 g) kosher salt, ¼ cup (30 g) black pepper, 4 teaspoons (9 g) paprika, 4 teaspoons (14 g) garlic powder, 2 teaspoons (5 g) onion powder, and 2 teaspoons (3.5 g) cayenne pepper (optional). Store in a glass jar with a lid in a cool, dry place. Makes about 1½ cups (350 g).

MEXICAN SEASONING

In a small bowl stir together ¾ cup (90 g) paprika, ⅓ cup (90 g) chili powder, ⅓ cup (15 g) dried oregano, 3 tablespoons (15 g) kosher salt, 3 tablespoons (15 g) ground cumin, 2 tablespoons (10 g) garlic powder, 2 tablespoons (10 g) onion powder, 1 tablespoon (5 g) ground coriander, and 2 teaspoons (3 g) black pepper. Store in a glass jar with a lid in a cool, dry place. Makes about 2 cups (255 g).

CHILI SEASONING

In a small bowl stir together 1 cup (135 g) chili powder, ⅓ cup (15 g) salt, ⅓ cup (15 g) ground cumin, 4 teaspoons (7 g) cayenne pepper, 4 teaspoons (7 g) garlic powder, 1 tablespoon (5 g) onion powder, and 1 tablespoon (5 g) black pepper. Store in a glass jar with a lid in a cool, dry place. Makes about 2 cups (190 g).

ITALIAN SEASONING

In a small bowl combine ¼ cup (20 g) dried basil, ¼ cup (20 g) dried oregano, 2 tablespoons (10 g) dried rosemary, ¼ cup (7 g) dried thyme, and ¼ cup (7 g) dried marjoram. Store in a glass jar with a lid in a cool, dry place. Makes about 1¼ cups (75 g).

BEEF AND BEAN CHILI

MAKES 9 PINTS

Few dishes warm you up on a cold day like chili, and this classic recipe is in heavy rotation in my kitchen during the colder months of the year. I even miss it enough in the summer to brave a batch every now and then. This recipe even gives you the chance to put your spice-blending skills to work, using your own homemade Mexican spice blend (instead of a store-bought chili seasoning packet). And I think the best part is that you perform the final cooking of the ingredients in a pressure canner, creating jars of chili that will last for years! Just heat them up and add a few fresh herbs and spices to revitalize the dish before serving.

3	cups (500 g) dried pinto or red kidney beans
5½	cups (1.3 l) water
2	teaspoons (10 g) salt
3	pounds (1.5 kg) ground beef or venison
1½	cups (80 g) chopped onion
1	cup (150 g) chopped red or green sweet peppers
¼	cup (60 ml) Mexican Seasoning (recipe, item 011)
2	quarts (2 l) crushed or whole tomatoes

1. Wash the jars and lids with hot, soapy water. Rinse well and place on a clean towel, open sides up, to dry. (Set screw bands aside.) Place the jars in a boiling-water canner and cover with hot water. Bring to a simmer over medium heat and boil for 10 minutes. Place lids in a small saucepan and cover with hot water. Bring to a simmer over medium heat (do not boil). Keep the jars and lids submerged in hot water, covered, until ready to use.

2. Wash beans thoroughly and place them in a large pot. Add cold water to reach 2 to 3 inches above the beans; soak beans 12 to 18 hours. Drain and discard water.

3. In the same pot combine the beans with the 5½ cups (1.3 L) water and the salt. Bring to boiling over medium-high heat. Reduce heat and simmer for 30 minutes. Drain and discard water.

4. Meanwhile, in batches, cook the ground meat, onion, and peppers in a large skillet until meat is browned and onion and peppers have softened. Drain any fat. Add the Mexican Seasoning, tomatoes, and beans. Cook over medium heat until heated through, about 5 minutes.

5. Using tongs, remove one jar at a time from hot water; pour water back into pot. Using a wide-mouth funnel, ladle chili into the hot jar to within 1-inch of the top. Tap jars on the table to remove air bubbles. Wipe the jar rims and place lids on jars; add screw bands and tighten just to fingertip tight.

6. Process jars according to the chart (opposite) for a dial-gauge pressure canner or weighted-gauge pressure canner.

RECOMMENDED PROCESS TIME FOR A DIAL-GAUGE PRESSURE CANNER

STYLE OF PACK	JAR SIZE	PROCESS TIME	PSI 0-2000 FT	PSI 2001-4000 FT	PSI 4001-6000 FT	PSI 6001-8000 FT
Hot	Pint	75 min	11 lb (4.9 kg)	12 lb (5.4 kg)	13 lb (5.9 kg)	14 lb (6.4 kg)

RECOMMENDED PROCESS TIME FOR A WEIGHTED-GAUGE PRESSURE CANNER

STYLE OF PACK	JAR SIZE	PROCESS TIME	PSI 0-1000 FT	PSI ABOVE 1000 FT
Hot	Pint	75 min	10 lb (4.5 kg)	15 lb (6.9 kg)

012 PLAN YOUR MEALS

Yes, you could probably live off a pallet of canned peaches, but after the thirty-third can, you may not want to. It's easy to add to your survival stockpile by throwing random things into the cupboard. But a better plan is just that: a plan.

Figure out some complete meals your family would gladly eat, then stock enough food to supply those meals. Some people even store their assorted menu items together.

Everything on this grocery list can be eaten right out of the package–just add a little hot water for the oatmeal–and it can create three days of meals for a family of four.

BREAKFAST The three breakfasts are the first things on the list. Granola and milk will make one breakfast meal, and the oatmeal will make two more. There's one extra packet at each meal for the hungriest survivor.

LUNCH AND DINNER Your lunches and dinners can be a rotation of soups, pastas, and chili, with vegetables on the side (or added to the meal). Add a can of tomatoes or corn to the chili and green beans or other veggies to your soups.

SNACKS The cookies and energy bars are there to fill in for dessert, eat as a snack, and keep everyone happy.

SHOPPING LIST

1	box instant oatmeal (10 packs, your favorite flavor)
1	package shelf-stable milk (3 Tetra pak blocks, 1 cup/236 ml each)
1	package granola
8	cans soup
12	cans prepared pasta (like ravioli)
12	cans vegetables
4	cans chili
1	tin butter cookies (or similar long-lasting treats)
1	box energy bars (12 bars)

013 MAKE SOME HARDTACK

What makes a good survival food? First, you need to be able to store it for long periods of time. Second, it needs to be nutritious. And third, it should taste good. Tasting good is not really a necessity, but it sure is nice if you end up living off the stuff for a long time.

Hardtack satisfies all three conditions. Once it's dried thoroughly, it will keep for years, provided it stays dry and away from pests. If you make it with natural, healthy ingredients, it's very nutritious. And if you know how to prepare it, it tastes delicious. Because it is completely dehydrated, it is relatively light and easy to transport, but because it is so dense, it packs a lot of nutrition in a small package.

Hardtack has actually been around since the time of Egyptian sailors, but you probably know it better from the Civil War period. During the war, squares of hardtack were shipped to both the Union and Confederate armies, making it a staple of a soldier's rations. Typically made six months beforehand, it was as hard as a rock when it actually got to the troops. To soften it, they usually soaked it in water or coffee. Not only would this soften it enough for eating, but any insect larvae in the bread would float to the top, allowing the soldiers to skim them out.

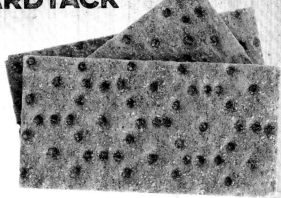

YOU'LL NEED
4 to 5 cups (480g–600 g) flour
2 cups (0.5 l) water
2 to 3 teaspoons (10g–15 g) salt

DIRECTIONS Mix the flour, water, and salt, making sure the mixture is fairly dry. Then roll it out to about ½-inch (1-cm) thickness, and shape into a rectangle. Cut it into 3x3-inch (8x8-cm) squares, and poke holes in both sides. Place on an ungreased cookie sheet, and bake for 30 minutes per side at 375°F (190°C).

014 PREPARE YOUR OWN PEMMICAN

An ancient forebear of the modern survival ration, pemmican was originally prepared by Native Americans as a traveling food and cold-weather snack. Traditional pemmican is a blend of dried meat pounded into a powder, then blended with warm animal fat and often supplemented with dried fruits, berries, or other available foods. This mixture can be rolled into balls, pressed into a loaf, or formed into cakes, and added to a pot of boiling water to make a greasy soup base.

YOU'LL NEED
8 ounces (0.2 kg) lard
1 8-ounce (0.2-kg) cup tightly packed with powdered jerky
8 ounces (0.2 kg) dried fruit
Flour, chopped nuts, and/or spices (optional)

GET READY The lard, jerky, and fruit are essential ingredients. Some folks add a little flour for extra carbs, a handful of chopped nuts for fat, or spices to make it taste a little better. Keep an eye on the temp–cold lard won't incorporate well with other ingredients, and melted lard will cook jerky slightly, leading to dangerous spoilage. Get lard to a soft state by warming slightly or stirring aggressively.

MIX IT UP Add the lard to a bowl containing all the other ingredients, and stir until well incorporated.

STORE IT Loosely wrap the pemmican in wax paper, and store it in a cool, dry, dark place. It can last for months before the fat turns rancid, especially in cold weather. Store it out of the reach of pests.

TUNA NOODLE CASSEROLE

SERVES 4

We get the word casserole from the diminutive form of casse, a French word meaning a "deep pan or bowl," though this food cannot be claimed solely by the Francs. It's a chimera of a dish with a more universal origin, likely dating back to the earliest stone bowls and earthenware dishes. The interchangeable mixture of meats, vegetables, and starches may have originally been baked by an open fire, then later in simple wood-fired ovens. By the late 1800s, the casserole begins to appear in a form we would find very familiar today. Both baked and served in the same dish, this filling food is a great way to use random staples, and you can incorporate any fresh ingredients you may have lying around. If you want a classic American take on this surprisingly ancient dish, look no further than tuna noodle casserole. With a bag of egg noodles, some tuna, and a can of soup, you've built the foundation. Then it's up to you (and your available ingredients) to vary the flavor and nutrition with add-ins such as cheese, pimiento, or frozen peas, or by topping the dish with crumbled potato chips.

8   ounces (224 g) wide egg noodles

3   tablespoons (15 g) butter, divided

½   medium (26 g) yellow onion, chopped

2   stalks celery, chopped

1   cup sliced mushrooms

½   teaspoon (2.5 g) salt
     Black pepper

1   (10.5-ounce) (310 ml) can cream of celery soup

½   cup (120 ml) milk

1   (6-ounce) (170 g) can water-packed tuna, drained and flaked

1   cup (80 g) shredded cheddar cheese

½   cup (40 g) grated Parmesan cheese, divided

1   tablespoon (15 ml) lemon juice

2   tablespoons (7.5 g) chopped fresh parsley or 2 teaspoons (1 g) dried parsley flakes

1   tablespoon (3 g) chopped fresh dill or 1 teaspoon (1 g) dried dill

1   tablespoon (3 g) chopped fresh chives or 1 teaspoon (1 g) dried chives

¼   cup (30 g) panko bread crumbs

1. Cook noodles according to package directions. Drain and set aside.

2. Preheat oven to 400°F (200°C). In a large, oven-going skillet melt 2 tablespoons (30 g) of the butter over medium heat. Add the onion, celery, and mushrooms, and cook, stirring occasionally, until slightly softened, about 5 minutes. Season with salt and pepper to taste.

3. Stir in soup and milk. Simmer for 2 to 3 minutes, stirring occasionally. Remove from heat. Stir in noodles, tuna, cheddar cheese, ¼ cup (20 g) of the Parmesan cheese, the lemon juice, parsley, dill, and chives.

4. Melt remaining 1 tablespoon (15 g) butter. In a small bowl combine melted butter, bread crumbs, and remaining ¼ cup (20 g) Parmesan cheese. Sprinkle over the noodle mixture in the skillet. Bake until bubbly and golden on top, 17 to 20 minutes.

WHITE RICE

1 EXERCISE BAGS If you're lucky enough to find a huge bag of rice at an international grocery store, you've got food for weeks at a bargain price. You've also got a way to work off all those empty carbs. An unopened sack of rice (any size) can be a great tool for simple exercises. Work on your grip strength by carrying it. Add weight to your body-weight squats by holding the bag to your core, squatting and then standing up straight again. Rest the bag on your back while doing pushups. Come up with your own exercise routines involving a heavy bag. And only use thick or reinforced bags, so you don't spill the precious contents.

2 DRYING ELECTRONICS When you consider all the nonfood uses for rice, the one that we tend to be the most emotional about is rice's ability to save our expensive smart phones and high-end electronics. After a trip into the sink or the toilet bowl, a large plastic bag full of dry white rice can exorcise the specter of moisture from your ailing device and bring it back to life. Just dry the surface of your phone or gadget and place it in a bag of rice. Leave it for several days. Waiting is the hardest part, but when the time comes, the rice has likely absorbed all the errant water and the phone should be functional again. Store a few more days, if not.

3 RICE FLOUR For those with a flour mill (or a mortar and pestle, and lots of time on their hands), ordinary white rice can be ground into an interesting gluten-free flour. It won't create chewy bread in the way that wheat flour can. The results tend to be more granular and less cohesive, more like cornbread. In any case, rice flour can be a stand alone baking ingredient or a great companion with other staples. You can use it as a fine thickener for soups and stews. It can also be transformed into cookies and crackers. You can even mix it with wheat flour for an interesting version of regular wheat bread.

4 RICE WINE AND BEER Rice wine is a catchall term for a wide range of alcoholic beverages made from rice and other cereals in Asia. Since many of these drinks are clear with the alcohol content of a fruit wine, the name "rice wine" has stuck. You could enjoy sake in Japan, shaosingjiu in China, and a related drink called makgeolli that resembles a cloudy beer (the oldest alcoholic drink in Korea, dating back over 2000 years). These world brews are some of the most consumed alcoholic drinks on earth, and with the right strains of *Saccharomyces cerevisiae* (yeast), you can join the long line of rice brewers (for fun or for survival).

5 THERAPY PACKS Dry white rice can hold heat or cold for some time, making it surprisingly good as a hot pack or cold pack for various maladies. For an easy therapy pack, grab a long tube sock made from tightly woven fabric (with no holes in the toe, otherwise the rice will pour out). Cotton fabric would be best, as you can heat it without the fear of melting (like synthetic fabric). Fill the sock with rice, and tie it shut (very securely). Microwave the sock full of rice for a minute or two, and check it for warmth. If you want it hotter, add another minute and apply to the injury. This sock of rice can also be frozen to serve as a great cold pack.

6 RUST PREVENTATIVE We can't have our tools and weapons rusting up! From tool boxes to gun safes, savvy survivors will add a cloth or paper bag full of dry white rice to their storage as a moisture absorber and rust preventative. It's important to use a breathable bag (not a plastic bag), as the rice will only absorb moisture when the exchange isn't blocked by a waterproof membrane. In more humid weather, replace the rice every few weeks to keep the moisture at bay. In drier weather, the rice will only need to be replaced every few months. And even though the rice may have soaked up moisture, it's still fine to eat.

7 **LIVESTOCK FEED** White rice can last a very long time just sitting in a cabinet in your home. Some rice may even get a little better with age (basmati rice is often likened to a fine wine, improving as it sits). But at some point, the Grim Reaper will catch up to your food storage (unless you packed it in Mylar with oxygen absorbers). When your rice is finally so old that it's taken on a stale or rank flavor, you can still cook up a batch and feed it to less discriminating palates. Chickens and pigs will be thrilled to get some rice. Just make sure it's cooked. Uncooked rice can be very harmful to animals, as it swells with water in their gut.

8 **TRADE GOOD** What's a big sack of rice worth after the apocalypse? It might be worth any price you'd ask. White rice has 100 calories an ounce, the same as pasta or wheat flour, making it a very valuable food resource that does not need refrigeration to store and only needs boiling water to prepare. While bigger is usually better in most arenas, you may want to go modular with your rice as a trade good for tough times. Smaller factory-sealed bags will look legitimate to your prospective trade partners and be easier to transport. Small bags will also be easier to assign a reasonable value (compared to high-value items).

9 **AMUSEMENTS** Entertainment doesn't rank up there with building a shelter as a survival priority. In a long-term crisis, however, distractions and amusements do have significant value. White rice could become a noise-making maraca for a kid with a little rice in a plastic bottle. That same bottle could also be a "treasure hunt" game, with more rice and a few trinkets inside. With a steady hand and a microscopic paintbrush, you could write someone's name on a grain of rice. For something more athletic, rice in a small bag could become a hacky sack for kicking or a ball for tossing around. Use your imagination and have fun!

10 **RICE MILK** Out of "moo juice" for your breakfast cereal? Rice can serve as the source of a milk-like beverage. Soak 3/4 cup (140 g) uncooked long grain white rice in 2 cups (480 ml) very hot water for two hours. Drain the partially softened rice and add it to a high-speed blender. Add 4 cups (1 l) water, a pinch of salt, and one or two pitted dates for sweetness. Blend for one solid minute, until the date bits are very small. Cover a bowl with a clean T-shirt and pour the blended mixture through it. You can add a few drops of vanilla extract for more flavor, and store this "milk" in a fridge for several days. Use as you would ordinary rice milk.

HEARTY HOMESTEAD BEAN AND RICE STEW

SERVES 6 TO 8

Not only are beans and rice a great combination for flavor and texture, they provide a complete protein! Individually, beans and rice provide us with seven of the nine essential amino acids (building blocks of protein that our bodies cannot create for themselves). Whether you choose brown rice or white rice, both are high in the amino acid methionine. When we add in the beans, we get plenty of lysine, another essential amino acid and one that's lacking in rice. Bring these two staple foods together, and you've got all the protein building blocks you need for a healthy diet. Just 1 cup (239 grams) of rice and beans dishes up 12 grams of complete protein (and 10 grams of tasty fiber). And when we combine these simple staple foods with a few other ingredients, you can create a dish that's both nutritious and delicious.

1	pound (0.5 kg) dried beans, such as navy, cannellini, kidney, and/or pinto beans (2 cups total) (480 ml), soaked overnight
10	cups (2.4 l) water
6	vegetable or chicken bouillon cubes
2	bay leaves
1	cinnamon stick
1	cup (185 g) long grain white rice
⅓	cup (30 g) chopped dried leeks or 1 cup (90 g) chopped fresh leeks
⅔	cup (50 g) diced dried carrots or 2 cups (250 g) diced fresh carrots
1	white onion, chopped or 1 tablespoon (15 g) onion powder
2	cloves garlic, minced, or 1 teaspoon (5 g) garlic powder
1	teaspoon (5 g) salt, plus more to taste
1	teaspoon (5 g) cracked black pepper
1	teaspoon (1.5 g) celery seed
½	to 1 teaspoon (0.5–1 g) crushed red pepper
1	teaspoon (1.5 g) ground cumin

1. Drain and rinse beans. Set aside.

2. In a large pot bring the water to boiling. Add bouillon cubes and stir to dissolve. Reduce heat; add beans, bay leaves, and cinnamon stick. Bring to boiling; reduce heat and simmer, uncovered for 1 hour, stirring occasionally. Remove and discard bay leaves and cinnamon stick.

3. Add rice to the pot. Simmer, stirring occasionally, until beans are almost tender and rice is cooked, about 30 minutes. (Add additional water, if needed, to reach desired consistency.)

4. Stir in leeks, carrots, onion, garlic, salt, black pepper, celery seed, crushed red pepper, and cumin. Cook until beans and vegetables are tender, stirring occasionally, 15 to 30 minutes more.

WHILE BROWN RICE DOESN'T LAST VERY LONG IN STORAGE, ANY KIND OF WHITE RICE LASTS FOR YEARS WHEN PROPERLY PACKAGED AND STORED. ANY OF THEM WILL WORK IN THIS ADAPTABLE RECIPE.

015 PLAN FOR THE LONG HAUL

Certain foods, if properly stored, can last up to 30 years or more in your pantry. Remember, do not try these long-term storage methods with even very slightly moist foods to avoid the risk of botulism.

STORE FOR UP TO 30 YEARS IN PETE BOTTLES: Wheat · White rice · Dried corn · White sugar · Pinto beans · Rolled oats · Dry pasta · Potato flakes · Nonfat powdered milk

NOT SUITABLE FOR LONG-TERM STORAGE: Pearled barley · Jerky · Nuts · Dried eggs · Brown rice · Whole-wheat flour · Milled grain · Brown sugar · Granola

Not sure if a foodstuff is dry enough? Try this test. Place it on a piece of paper and whack it with a hammer. If it shatters, it's dry. If it squishes, it definitely isn't. And if it breaks but leaves a little spot of water or oil, it's still too moist. Err on the side of safety–your family's life is literally on the line.

016 GET THE MOST FROM A PROPANE STOVE

Propane stoves are a great convenience for cooking when you're in the wilderness, off the grid, or making do while waiting for power to come back. But they are designed for small tanks, which run out quickly, are annoying to store, and are costly. Luckily, you can buy an adapter from camping stores or often directly from the stove's maker that will allow you to hook up a 5-gallon tank instead. The adapters are cheap, and the bigger tanks are a great bargain and can last for months. (For those seven people in the world who have never been camping, you can cook just about anything on a propane stove that you'd cook on your regular indoor range.)

017 MUNCH ON MRES, IF YOU MUST

MREs have definitely taken up space in the civilian market, above and beyond the leftover stockpiles that you might find at a military surplus store. MRE stands for "Meals Ready to Eat," though a more fitting description might be a "pouch of pouches." These bulky brown bags are a little on the expensive side, and they only last a few years (under ideal conditions), but they provide no-cook meals that are ready to eat, as advertised. The MRE was first rolled out as a test ration for the U.S. military in 1975. Over the next 15 years, the menu was tested, many items were replaced, hot sauce was added, and candy and cold beverages were included. The first major military reliance on MRE meals came with Operation Desert Storm in 1990, and the MRE

has continued to change, matching the tastes and needs of consumers. The "chili and macaroni" meal is one of the most coveted selections from the current menu, while chicken ala king (which was discontinued) was widely known as the worst MRE ever (dubbed chicken ala death by disenchanted diners). Several different companies manufacture these meals in the U.S., and there are many other providers worldwide. Most MREs contain roughly 1,400 calories, so two of these pouches can provide all of the necessary daily calories for an active adult. Menu options abound, though most manufacturers sell them in mixed cases of twelve. To turn two of these MREs into three square meals, open up two pouches and take inventory of all the entrées

and snacks. Decide which items you'll have for breakfast, lunch, and dinner, and trade any unwanted items with your buddies. If you're really lucky (or you planned ahead by buying the right products), your MREs will include a water-activated chemical heater packet, which will heat up one entrée in about 10 minutes.

018 SURVIVAL KITCHEN ITEMS

1 DISH SOAP Dish soap isn't just for dishes. I've used it to wash my hands, degrease animal hides, wash my hair and body, and perform many other useful tasks. There are plenty of types of dish soap to choose from. Antibacterial ones are great for sanitizing, and the degreasing kind, well, you already know what they do.

2 WIRE RACK You may have loose wire racks that you use for drying dishes or cooking baked goods, or you may steal one of the wire racks from your oven. In a grid-down setting with the utilities out, those wire racks can be suspended over a fire in the backyard, and you'll be able to resume your "normal" cooking chores.

3 FIRE EXTINGUISHER Sure, you could spray this in a home invader's face or use the canister like a big hammer to crack open walnuts, but the intended use of this item is so important, it's a must-have kitchen survival item. Since most house fires start in the kitchen, keeping an extinguisher nearby can be a lifesaving decision.

4 HAND TOWELS Hand towels aren't just a sustainable alternative to paper towels. These absorbent fabric pieces can be improvised bandages, filters, storage bags, padding, and any of the thousand other uses for a simple piece of fabric. Let your imagination guide your creativity. These are more than just a one-trick pony.

5 PLASTIC BAGS Keep the dry stuff dry and keep the air out for storage. An assortment of freezer-thickness and regular-thickness ziptop plastic bags in various sizes can be great for everyday kitchen uses. They can also keep your tinder dry, ration your food into serving sizes, and preform dozens of other survival tasks.

6 FIRE STARTERS Any self-respecting kitchen junk drawer should have a box of matches and butane lighter. These aren't just handy for lighting little birthday cake candles. They can light stoves and anything else we need to ignite in an emergency. Keep multiple fire starters handy, but out of the reach of your pyro children.

7 BIG KNIFE Whether you have a chef's knife, a meat cleaver, or you just like to chop your carrots with a Bowie knife, a large sharp cutting tool is a necessary part of your kitchen hardware. It can also be a weapon. And if you can manage to keep it sharp, it'll be more than just frightening–it will be effective.

8 ALUMINUM FOIL Not only can aluminum foil make a great hat (which keeps the aliens and the government from reading your mind), it's also great for cooking and wrapping up food. A foil-wrapped packet of food can be baked in the oven or on the coals of a fire. Foil-wrapped leftovers will be protected from flies and dust. This malleable metal product can even conduct electricity, making it suitable for all kinds of science projects.

9 STOCKPOT A big stockpot can do more than turn water into broth. Stockpots are great for boiling larger volumes of water to disinfect it. You can also cook large meals for groups, and use them as buckets for hauling water or other substances. With tight-fitting lids, they can even be used for mouse-proof storage.

10 VODKA Vodka can make you sick as a dog when you overindulge on the cheap stuff. It can get you drunk as hell when you overindulge on the cheap or top-shelf stuff. It can also be used as a (painfully stinging) disinfectant for wounds, as a medicine to help you sleep, as a fire-starting fuel, and much more.

KOREAN MARINADE AND SAUCE

MAKES ABOUT 1½ CUPS

Bulgogi (pronounced "bull-GO-ghee") is one of my favorite meals! It's thinly sliced beef marinated in a sweet sauce that seems nothing short of heaven-sent. This divine dish is often referred to as Korean barbecue, though the meat is typically fried (not smoked or grilled). It's a beloved dish in Korea, and as more people learn about this magical meat entrée, it's becoming very popular worldwide. So what's the secret? It's the sauce. Bulgogi sauce can be used as a meat marinade prior to cooking your Korean barbecue. It can also be (and should be) used to dip the beef strips (or any other meat) after cooking. Some bulgogi sauces are thick, with a glaze-like texture. Other recipes produce a sauce that is quite thin and watery, like a North Carolina style barbecue sauce. However it's made, this sauce provides a unique and savory blend of salty soy, sweetness, and tanginess with garlicky and spicy notes throughout. Not only is this sauce perfect for beef, it can used like any other barbecue sauce. It's also a great addition to stir-fries and fried rice. And as with any sauce, interesting variations are yours for the creation. Make a spicier bulgogi sauce by adding more chile pepper flakes or chile paste. Increase the sweetness with honey for those with a sweet tooth. Make this sauce your own.

1   cup (240 ml) soy sauce

¼   cup (30 g) finely chopped dried pear

3   tablespoons (50 g) honey

2   tablespoons (30 ml) gochujang (fermented red pepper paste)

1   tablespoon (15 ml) toasted sesame oil

2   tablespoons (10 g) dried minced garlic

2   teaspoons (10 g) dried ground ginger

1   teaspoon (1 g) crushed red pepper flakes

1   teaspoon (1 g) cracked black pepper

1. Combine all of the ingredients in a medium saucepan. Bring to a simmer over medium heat. Cook, stirring occasionally, until thickened slightly, 5 to 10 minutes. Cool completely. Store in airtight container in the refrigerator for up to 2 weeks.

To use as a marinade: Place beef or pork in a large resealable plastic bag. Pour ½ cup (120 ml) marinade over the meat and turn to coat. Seal the bag; marinate in the refrigerator for at least 3 hours or up to overnight. When ready to cook, shake off excess marinade. Lightly coat the meat with neutral oil and cook over an open flame. Or cook meat in a small amount of oil in a hot skillet.

To use as a sauce: In a saucepan simmer the sauce over medium heat until reduced by half. Serve over cooked meat. (For a smoother sauce, use a fine-mesh strainer to remove pear and garlic pieces.)

Note: Sliced green onions and toasted sesame seeds make a delicious garnish on dishes made with this marinade/sauce.

019 FIGURE OUT HOW MUCH WATER YOU'LL NEED

Survival guides will tell you to store enough water for a week or more, but how do you know what that means? Look at the figures below, then multiply the daily numbers by 14 for adults, children, elderly, infants, and the sick or wounded to calculate your family's water storage requirements for a two-week emergency.

ACTIVITY LEVEL	BARE BONES	SOME ACTIVITY	DRY CLIMATE OR VERY ACTIVE	DRY CLIMATE AND VERY ACTIVE
Ill, Burned, or Wounded Adult	2 gal (8 l)	3 gal (11 l)	4 gal (15 l)	5 gal (19 l)
Average Adult	1 gal (4 l)	1.5 gal (6 l)	2 gal (8 l)	3 gal (11 l)
Children & Elderly	0.75 gal (3 l)	1 gal (4 l)	2 gal (8 l)	2 gal (8 l)
Infants	0.5 gal (2 l)	1 gal (4 l)	1.5 gal (6 l)	2 gal (8 l)

020 RESPECT THE CHEMICALS

You may remember the old ad that reminded us that without chemicals, life would be impossible. That's true. But it's also true that if you don't properly respect and understand the chemicals you're working with, you can do yourself a world of harm. Consider the following when disinfecting water:

TAKE YOUR TIME This is powerful stuff, so don't rush it. Never take shortcuts with water safety; it's worth doing right. After all, the last thing you need in an emergency situation is a case of dysentery on top of everything else.

KEEP IT SIMPLE Never mix chemicals when disinfecting water. Choose one method and stick to it, as some mixtures can be dangerous.

KNOW THE RISKS Avoid using iodine to purify water if anyone who will be drinking it is pregnant or nursing, or has thyroid problems.

BE EFFICIENT Counterintuitively, tincture of iodine 2% is actually much stronger than the 10% povidone iodine solution that's sold as a disinfecting agent, so you'll use less of it. An added benefit to any iodine product is that you can use iodine for wound disinfection (never use chlorine for this!).

021 HARVEST THE RAIN

One of the most obvious sources of water is what falls from the sky. You shouldn't make rainwater the linchpin of your strategy, but if you live in an area that gets a decent amount of rain, it can't hurt to take advantage of this, er, windfall.

Some areas have laws against collecting rainwater, generally targeted at those who divert large amounts that would have fed into reservoirs (most common in drought-plagued Western states), so look into local ordinances.

A kiddie pool is a good vessel; it'll collect about 18 gallons (69 liters) in a modest rainfall. You can also place buckets beneath your downspouts to collect water that runs off the roof.

All water gathered using these methods should be purified before drinking–even "pure" rainwater can have contaminants.

022 HOLD YOUR WATER

Water is a top survival priority, so get the right containers to fulfill this necessity.

GALLON JUGS Glass wine jugs or juice jugs can be a nice choice for household storage–until you break them. Plastic 1-gallon (4-l) water jugs are more resistant to breakage, but they are vulnerable to leakage and chewing rodents. Don't reuse milk and juice jugs, as they're hard to sanitize and often grow more bacteria.

WATER BOB This 100-gallon (400-l) water bladder can be laid in a bathtub and filled from the tub's faucet in 20 minutes. It's a great thing to deploy if you know that trouble is coming, such as a hurricane heading for you.

SODA BOTTLES It's totally okay to use reclaimed 2-liter soda bottles. Make sure the containers are stamped with HDPE (high-density polyethylene) and coded with the recycle symbol and a number 2 inside. HDPE containers are FDA-approved for food and water storage.

WATER COOLER JUGS The Holy Grail of water containers, the 5-gallon (19-l) cooler jug can hold a lot of water and stay portable. Buy them factory-filled; they'll be safe to drink for a year or more.

55-GALLON (210-L) DRUMS Designed specifically for water storage, these big blue monsters will hold a week's worth of water or more. But they can be difficult to transport if you have to move them when full. Make sure it's a food-grade water barrel. Other barrels may create chemical interactions between the water and the plastic.

023 THINK OUTSIDE THE SINK

It doesn't take much to disrupt municipal water–earthquakes can break pipes, floods can overwhelm the system, and so forth.

And sometimes it takes the city awhile to get the taps back on. If the water stops flowing to your home, you do have a few options to consider before you start sucking on your last ice cubes. There's abundant water hidden in the average dwelling, if you know where to look for it.

THE PIPES Even in a utility outage, water can be found lying in the pipes. Open the highest faucet in the house, then open the lowest faucet or spigot, catching the water in some clean containers.

THE WATER HEATER You may find 40 to 80 gallons (150 to 300 liters) of drinkable water simply by opening the drain valve at the bottom of the unit and catching the water in a pan or shallow dish. Use this water soon, as warm water is a great bacterial breeding ground. Turn off the power to electric water heaters, as they will burn up with no water in the unit.

THE TOILET TANK To clarify, we are talking about the tank, not the toilet bowl. The tank of every toilet has a gallon (4 l) or more of perfectly clean water in it.

THE FISH TANK A freshwater fish tank can be claimed as a water source, along with koi ponds, fountains, and other water features. Treat this water with chemicals or by boiling for 10 minutes to make it safe to drink.

THE GUTTERS The gutter system on your home can provide many gallons of water from a light rain. Divert downspouts into rain barrels or other large containers

024 LET THE SUN SHINE IN

If you have a clear glass or plastic bottle, some water, and a sunny day, you can use the sun's light to make your water much safer to drink. Largely advocated for developing countries, solar water disinfection is gaining some traction in the survival-skills crowd. And it's a great fit for equatorial countries with abundant strong sunlight but few other resources.

The most common solar disinfection technique is to expose clear plastic bottles full of questionable water to the sun for a minimum of one day. The sun's abundant UV light kills or damages almost all biological hazards in the water. This method has many advantages: It's easy to use, it's inexpensive or free, and it offers good (but not complete) bacterial and viral disinfection.

There are some problems though. You need sunny weather (or two days of overcast sky) to reach the maximum effectiveness. You cannot use it in rainy weather. It offers no residual disinfection. It may be less effective against bacterial spores and cyst stages of some parasites. Both the water and the bottle need to be very clear. And finally, it only works with bottles that are 2 liters or smaller.

While solar disinfection isn't 100 percent effective, it's still a lot better than taking your chances by drinking raw water.

025 BANISH BACTERIA

As unlikely as this may sound, you can actually disinfect your drinking water safely and effectively with common household items. Just be aware that chemical disinfection doesn't remove salt, toxins, or fallout–it just kills the living pathogens that would make you sick.

FILTER Any water you get from a rain barrel, your pool, or a nearby creek should be considered contaminated and in need of disinfection. Water that is visibly dirty or muddy should be filtered through a coffee filter or a cloth. This won't make it safe to drink, but it will help the following disinfection methods to work more effectively.

CHLORINE BLEACH Add 2–4 drops of ordinary chlorine bleach per quart (or liter) of water. Use 2 drops if the water is warm and clear. Go to 4 drops if it is very cold or murky. Put the bottle cap back on and shake the container for a minute. Then turn the bottle upside down and unscrew the cap a turn or two. Let a small amount of water flow out to clean the bottle threads and cap. Screw the lid back on tight, and wipe the exterior of the bottle to get the chlorine on all surfaces. Let it sit for one hour in a dark place and it will be ready to drink.

TINCTURE OF IODINE Use 5–10 drops of tincture of iodine 2% in one quart (or liter) of water. Flush the threads, wipe down the bottle, and allow it to sit in the shade one hour, as with chlorine. Use 5 drops tincture of iodine for clear warm water, and up to 10 drops for the cold or cloudy variety of water.

POVIDONE IODINE You'll need 8–16 drops per quart (or liter) of water with this form of iodine. Add 8 drops for nice-looking water and 16 drops for swamp water. Clean the bottle threads and wait an hour, as with the other methods.

026 DISINFECT WITH UV LIGHT

One of the most recent innovations in water disinfection is the portable UV light purifier. This device doles out a lethal dose of ultraviolet light, which kills or wounds many different types of waterborne pathogens. There are two main types of UV purifiers to choose from:

UV PENS These little pocket-size UV purifiers typically run on two AA batteries and work with push-button ease. To use, stick the light element into a glass of water. Hit the button and a 45-second cycle of glowing blue light will begin. The light bulb should be stirred through the water. In most cases, the water should be safe for immediate drinking. If the water was slightly cloudy, zap it a second time.

UV HAND-CRANK MODELS What if the power's out? There are hand-crank UV purifiers that provide disinfection with just a minute of manual labor. Fill the water bottle (in the kit) from your local source. Screw the bottle onto the device's housing and flip it. Crank the handle until the LED light turns green (about 90 seconds). Flip it again, unscrew the bottle, wipe the threads clean, and repeat.

027 KEEP CLEAR

Any cloudiness or significant solids in water will create hiding places for bacteria and other tiny vermin to elude the burning light of a UV device. This can mean that multiple doses of UV light still cannot properly disinfect the water, so make sure you use only clear water with any UV method.

028 DISINFECT BY BOILING WATER

Boiling water before drinking may seem like a labor-intensive and antiquated method of removing any biological contaminants from a questionable source. In many cases, however, this old-school trick is still the most effective option–killing 100% of the organisms that would cause you to become ill–without chemicals or special equipment.

HEAT SOURCE Any form of fire

byproduct of some other activity, such as a wood stove in your household, or the engine block of your running car.

BOILING CONTAINERS Metal and even some glass containers can handle the heat. Make sure the container is a safe material and set up in a sturdy way. You can boil water in pots, pans, cans, and other metal containers, but avoid galvanized metal, which imparts

even use glass bottles if you place them on the edge of the fire or heat source.

BOIL TIME Ten minutes of actual boiling temperatures will give you a much safer window of disinfection than the often-recommended one or two minutes. Start your count when the first big bubbles start to jump to the water's surface. Continue to boil, then let cool

FRUIT LEATHER

MAKES ABOUT 12 FRUIT ROLL-UPS

Fruit Roll-Ups and other commercially produced fruit leather strips are a popular dried fruit snack here in the U.S., though they have roots that reach deep into Old World history. Many people believe the first fruit leather was made in the Middle East, likely from pureed, cooked, and dried apricot. In the old days, this was a great way to take a briefly available seasonal produce (like a quick-spoiling fruit) and preserve it for year-round use. Today, we can make fruit leather for the same reason (to preserve a fleeting food resource). We can also make it because it's a delicious alternative to candy and other low-nutrition sweet snack foods. Fruit leathers can be produced in the traditional way, drying cooked and pureed fruit on a nonstick surface in dry, sunny weather. We can also take advantage of modern resources like ovens and dehydrators, if we have the utilities to operate them for reliable food-drying. You can even add your own vitamin supplements, like powdered citric acid (vitamin C), which will enhance the nutritional value of the food and act as a natural preservative. Take a chance at making your own fruit leather with your favorite fruit and our easy recipe.

4	cups (750 g) chopped fresh fruit, such as apricots, peaches, plums, berries, apples, pears, and/or grapes
½	cup (120 ml) water
1	tablespoon (15 ml) lemon juice
½	tablespoon (2.5 g) ground cinnamon (optional)
¼	teaspoon (0.5 g) ground nutmeg (optional)
	Sugar (optional)

1. Before chopping, wash fruit and remove any stems, pits, and thick peels.

2. In a blender or food processor combine fruit and the water; blend until smooth. Add lemon juice, cinnamon, and nutmeg, if using. Add sugar to taste, if needed.

3. Transfer fruit puree to a large saucepan. Cook over medium heat, stirring occasionally, until slightly thickened, 10 to 15 minutes.

4. Line dehydrator trays with parchment paper. Spread fruit puree over the parchment, about ¼ inch (6 mm) thick around the edges and ⅛ inch (3 mm) in center.

5. Dry fruit puree at 145°F (63°C) for 6 to 8 hours or until no longer sticky. Let cool completely before removing from the trays.

6. Roll the fruit leather into a tight roll and cut to desired lengths; wrap in plastic wrap. Store in airtight containers in a cool, dark place or vacuum-seal.

Oven directions: Preheat oven to 140°F (60°C). (Turn convection on, if available.) Place parchment paper on a large baking sheet. Spread fruit puree on the parchment. Dry fruit puree for 8 to 10 hours or until no longer sticky.

CAN'T GET YOUR KIDS TO EAT FRUIT? CONCENTRATE THE NATURAL SUGAR BY TRANSFORMING IT INTO THIS SWEET TREAT.

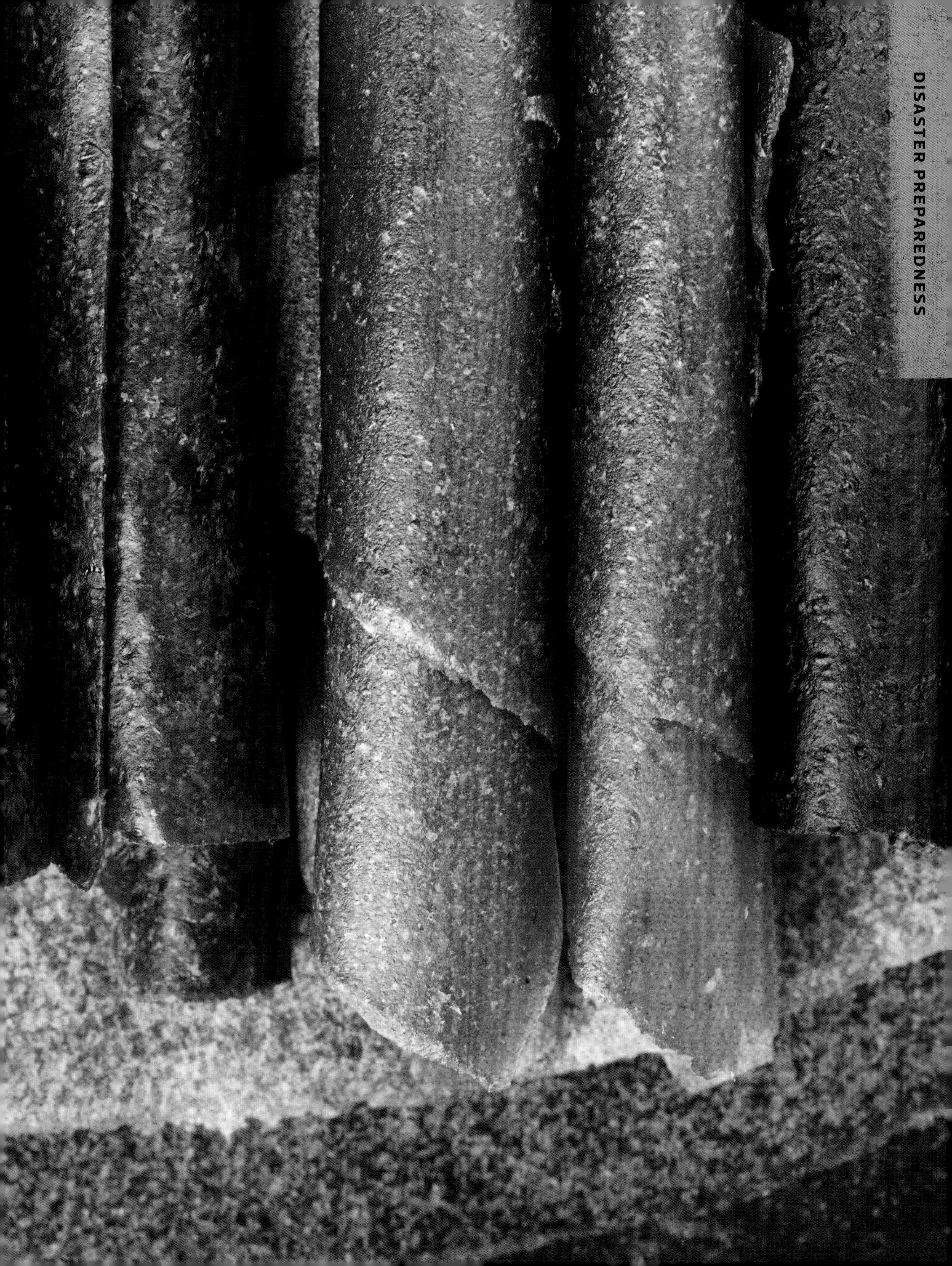

029 GO CUCKOO FOR COCONUT

Coconut water seems to be the trendy beverage of the moment. Thing is–for once–those hipsters may be onto something. Coconuts are amazingly healthy and versatile, and they have a special place in your pantry (and medical kit!).

OIL One problem with storing oils in a long-term survival pantry is that most oils go bad really fast, especially in the heat. Coconut oil lasts for up to two years without going rancid and, because it's solid at room temperature, doesn't need to be refrigerated. That all sound good? Well not only can you cook with it, it's a great skin moisturizer and has been touted as a topical cure for pink eye and even head lice.

WATER Coconut water is high in electrolytes and great for hydration. Store single-serving cans or pouches for a quick, refreshing treat after exertion in the hot sun. As a bonus, this will help you preserve your water stores for other purposes.

MILK Coconut milk is rich in taste and calories, and a delicious addition to rice, stews, and soups. Use it instead of water to boil your rice and not only will it taste better, it will also cook more quickly.

030 DRY OUT YOUR FRUITS

Fruits and vegetables are essential to a healthy diet, but dried fruit has a lot of sugar. Don't let that deter you; instead of avoiding dried fruit due to high sugar content, moderate your intake by eating it mixed with nuts for a trail mix, or with healthier, low-sugar foods like yogurt. Also, remember that in a survival situation, calories are your friends.

Once you've selected your fresh fruit, thoroughly wash it and make sure it's free of marks and blemishes. (If you are not sure what fruits are best to use for dehydrating, just take a trip to your local market and see what's common.) Then pit and slice the fruit accordingly. If you're drying larger berries, make sure to cut them in half.

With your fruit prepared, it's time to pretreat it. Most store-bought dried goods use sulfur to maintain color throughout the dehydrating process. You can skip the sulfur by creating a bath of ascorbic acid. You want 2 tablespoons (30 g) ascorbic acid for every quart or liter of water. And if you don't have ascorbic acid on hand, crush vitamin C tabs (you'll want 5 g).

If you live in a very hot environment, use the sun. Line a cookie sheet with cheesecloth, then lay out the fruit and let dry in the sun. Bring it in overnight to keep it from forming dew.

If you want to use your oven, keep it at its lowest setting, making sure internal temperatures don't rise above 145°F (63°C). Keep the oven door slightly ajar to allow any steam or moisture to escape. Drying times vary by fruit, so monitor closely. Successfully dried fruit should be leathery and not brittle to the touch.

031 BUILD A DEHYDRATOR

Food dehydrators are easily available as a kitchen appliance–but they're not much use when the power's out. And anyway, there's just something cool about growing your own tomatoes and making sun-dried snacks right there in the same backyard. Dried fruits and veggies are long-lasting and great for perking up dreary winter meals when the growing season's over. Here's how to make your own solar-powered snack machine.

YOU'LL NEED

3 **Three cardboard boxes**
Box knife
Black paint or black plastic sheeting
Clear plastic wrap
4 **dowels that are at least 2 inches (5 cm) longer than your box is wide**
Cloth screen, enough to make two shelves and to cover the box
Duct tape

STEP 1 Gather your cardboard boxes–they can be any size, provided they fit together nicely, as shown (you can make as many shelves as you like).

STEP 2 Cut one box down to be your reflection tray, or use the lid from a banker's box or similar. Cut ventilation holes in the two long sides, and paint its interior black, or coat in black plastic sheeting, then cover in clear plastic.

STEP 3 Cut holes through your large box, and thread through dowels as shown. Stretch screen over them and tape down firmly.

STEP 4 Cut a vent in the bottom of your larger box, and use duct tape to attach the reflection tray, so the sun's heat flows into the interior.

STEP 5 Set the main box on a second box to elevate it (you can also place it on a small table or chair). Angle the reflector so as to collect maximum sunlight.

STEP 6 Add fruit or veggies, and cover the box with more screening. Your fruit is done when it has a leathery texture; vegetables when they become brittle.

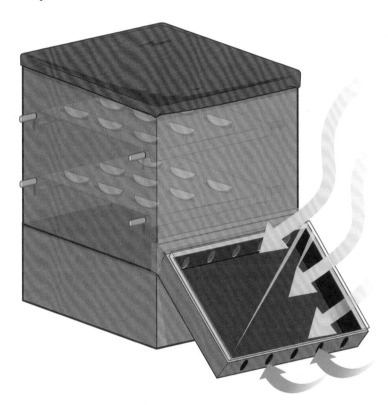

032 DRY IT IN THE DARK

If you live in a region where a solar dehydrator just won't get it done thanks to weather, sunshine, or humidity patterns, consider these old-school, sunshine-free drying techniques instead.

HANG 'EM UP Thread peeled, seeded, and sliced pieces of fruit or veggies onto a sturdy cotton string, cover with a thin cloth to keep off flies and dust, and hang above a radiator or stove top.

HIDE YOUR HERBS Herbs shouldn't be dried in the sun anyway, so for those of you shrouded in gloom and darkness, find a dry, dark place in the house, tie the stems into bouquets, and hang upside down.

033 EAT RIGHT IN A BLACKOUT

A power outage suddenly reduces your stove top to mere counter space and makes your refrigerator no better for food storage than a pantry. But you've still got to eat.

MIND THE EXPIRATION DATE Open the refrigerator door only when necessary to keep perishables and frozen food fresh. Usually food in the fridge is edible for a day, and food in the freezer for a couple of days.

IMPROVISE A FRIDGE If it looks like the power will be out for days, or (gulp) weeks, you can store your perishable foods in camp coolers or on blocks of ice in the bathtub.

COOK SAFELY Never fire up a grill or hibachi or start an open fire in the house. Instead, cook outdoors on a propane grill or using a Dutch oven and briquettes. If your fireplace is equipped with an iron-top inset, you can cook on that.

APPLY THE SNIFF TEST Discard unsafe foods that have a foul odor, color, or texture. Even when you're hungry, fuzz growing on the food is a bad sign.

034 TRIAGE YOUR FRIDGE AND FREEZER

When the power goes out, the food, drinks, and other items in your fridge and freezer won't last forever. You'll have a limited window of time where things will stay cold or frozen, and you may not be able to salvage everything. Start your grid-down damage control by creating a plan well before you open the fridge or freezer door. Try to remember every item you might have in there, and come up with a menu that will use the most vulnerable perishables in the next meal or two. Typically, your fresh meats and dairy are the most prone to spoilage, followed by cut fruit, bagged salads, and sliced vegetables. Intact produce, like heads of lettuce, whole fruits, and other uncut plant foods, should last longer. Plan what you'll grab to make the next meal, and get it out quickly when you are ready to cook that meal. Every second that the fridge or freezer door is open, precious cold air is drifting out onto your floor. While you're in there, you could remove anything from the fridge that can last in the open air (like your soy sauce and ketchup bottles), though you can also leave them in place. Their mass and cold temperature will help the fridge stay cool longer. And as you eat your rapidly melting ice cream, consider turning it into a milkshake or using the last scoop of melting ice cream as creamer for your coffee (see next page for more on coffee). Finally, cook or dehydrate anything you can, and keep those fridge and freezer doors closed. Everything will stay colder without the door being constantly opened and closed.

035 BREW COFFEE IN AN EMERGENCY

Even if you're short on electricity, you still need to get up and at 'em in the morning. But how, without your favorite electric grinder and espresso machine? Here are a few ways to get your morning joe.

COWBOY Rough-grind your coffee beans with a hand grinder or mortar and pestle, then throw them into a pot of water. Heat to simmering, then let cool as the grounds settle before pouring off the coffee (optional: use a filter to remove loose grounds).

TURKISH To make Turkish coffee, also known as mud coffee, grind your beans into a fine powder, then add to water. Bring to a boil, then remove from the heat. A layer of foam covers the top of the coffee, and the fine grounds sink to the bottom.

FRENCH PRESS You can find French presses made of sturdy plastic instead of costly glass. Add grounds and boiled water, steep for a few minutes, then press the sieve down to filter.

VIETNAMESE Place grounds in a small single-serve metal filter, then pour hot water over them. The coffee seeps through the filter into a cup below.

036 CONCENTRATE YOUR OWN COLD BREW

A few decades ago, no one had even heard of cold brew coffee. Coffee was brewed with heat and served hot. Now, however, cold brew coffee has a loyal fan base. Compared to the traditional hot cup of joe in the previous tip, cold brew coffee packs a vibrate-through-walls wallop. In the last several years, this concentrated wonder beverage has become a common sight at coffee houses both large and small. But don't worry about buying barista-grade aprons, expensive extraction equipment, fancy filters, or laboratory glassware to make this stuff. All you need is a solid container, water, coffee, and some plain coffee filters. As they said in the movie *Black Hawk Down*: "It's all in the grind." The coffee beans should be a medium to coarse grind, depending on your grinder. Add ⅓ cup (30 g) ground coffee to every 1 cup (240 ml) pure filtered water in a clean glass jar or similar container (or in a French press). Place the container in your refrigerator for at least 12 hours, though 24 hours is better. After the time has passed, strain your coffee through a coffee filter, or strainer, or by using the plunger on your French press. Your drink is now done, and it may contain as much as twice the normal caffeine of hot brewed coffee from the same ratio of ingredients. Drink your cold brew coffee straight, dilute it with water, or blend in other ingredients for a specialty beverage (and enjoy responsibly).

037 KEEP YOUR COOL

Without the gentle hum of the modern electric refrigerator, fresh meat spoils, dairy goes rancid, and produce can wilt or molder–some of which can be lost within a matter of hours. Refrigeration has become an essential cornerstone for the storage of many popular foodstuffs, but in a survival or disaster setting with power loss, these high-tech appliances will fail. The best defense against losing a large (and expensive)

volume of food is pre-gaming for a power outage. Don't overfill your freezer with items that you can't cook or eat quickly during a utility outage. Instead, fill your freezer with containers of water, which will freeze to become ice blocks. These can be transferred to the top shelf of your refrigerator during an outage to keep the fridge at a cooler temperature. As these containers of ice melt, you can use them for an emergency water source. Another option for those with a small amount of food and ice is to use a cooler. For cold storage in a non-winter situation, you can keep food cool temporarily in a cooler with ice. While the size, weight, and volume of the cooler will be important considerations, its easier to cool a small space than a large one. As a final option, you can take advantage of Mother Nature's refrigeration, cold weather. You can limit or even avoid some food loss in these circumstances by keeping your food in a chilly location in winter, like an unheated room or garage. And if the food can freeze solid and stay that way, it could last for a long time.

038 DON'T GET (FREEZER) BURNED

Food storage, especially for survival, only works well if the food is edible and palatable. So even though freezing food may preserve it for a very long time, the sneaking scourge of "freezer burn" can affect the taste, quality, and nutritional value of frozen foods (especially meat and produce). That effect known as freezer burn is a change in the condition of frozen food, typically caused when food is not packaged securely in airtight containers or wrappings. It's essentially a combination of dehydration and oxidation. When too much air reaches an improperly packaged frozen food, meat can appear to grow gray or brown spots with a shriveled texture. Starting at the surface and delving deeper into the frozen food, freezer burn changes more than just the pigment of a food. It dries the food, toughening the texture and creating an unfavorable flavor. Even though freezer-burned food has not become dangerous to eat, these dry spots make the food unpalatable and undesirable. Cutting away the obvious damaged areas will improve the food's quality, but it's still less desirable than it once was. Prevention is a much tastier route than

damage control, so make sure you block as much air from getting to your frozen food as possible. Double-wrap or triple-wrap your meats and vegetables that are destined for the freezer. Check your frozen food every few weeks for color changes. Rotate your frozen food and enjoy it before it turns to dry-yet-mushy and nearly inedible mess (though it's technically safe for human consumption).

NO-CHURN ICE CREAM

MAKES 12 SERVINGS (6 CUPS)

Who doesn't love ice cream? Aside from a few naysayers (probably with cold-sensitive teeth), most people adore this frigid food for its richness and beguiling combination of sweetness and fat. The first recognizable ice cream recipe appeared in 16th-century England as an evolution from the development of sherbet (a recipe brought back to Italy from the East by Marco Polo). A treat known as "cream ice" began to appear regularly on the table for King Charles I, and it eventually worked its way around the world and down from royal tables to the common folk. Today, the average American eats more than 23 pounds (10 kg) of ice cream annually, with over 1 billion gallons (4 billion liters) of ice cream and related treats being produced in the U.S. each year. Honestly, if someone invented a high-protein ice cream with vitamins, minerals, and fiber—I'm sure there'd be people living exclusively on this beloved frozen food. So what happens when you've scraped the last frosty bits from the bottom of the ice cream tub? You'd better know how to make an ice cream-adjacent confection that can satisfy your sweet tooth. Here's a way to do it without a specialized ice cream churning machine.

1   **(14-ounce) (392 g) can sweetened condensed milk**

2   **teaspoons (10 ml) vanilla extract**

2   **cups (480 ml) cold heavy cream**

1½   **cups (285 g) fresh blueberries or quartered strawberries, or 1 cup (170 g) coarsely chopped chocolate (optional)**

1. Line a 9x5-inch (23x13-cm) loaf pan with parchment paper. Place pan in the freezer.

2. In a large bowl whisk together the sweetened condensed milk and vanilla.

3. In another large bowl beat the cream with a mixer on medium-high until stiff peaks form (tips stand straight), about 2 minutes. Fold the whipped cream into the sweetened condensed milk. Pour into the chilled pan. Cover with plastic wrap and freeze until thick and creamy, about 2 hours. If desired, gently swirl in fruit or chocolate with a spoon. Cover and freeze until solid, 3 to 4 hours more.

"FAT IS THE CHARIOT UPON WHICH
FLAVOR RIDES." T.M.

ONE OF MY STUDENTS ONCE ASKED ME WHY
FAT WAS SO IMPORTANT, AND THAT WAS MY
INSPIRED REPLY. FAT IS JUST ONE REASON
ICE CREAM TASTES GREAT. THERE'S ALSO THE
SUGAR, FLAVORINGS, AND COLD CREAMINESS.

039 GO URBAN

Living in the city doesn't mean you can't grow a garden. There's always a way to make the room that you need to develop a supplemental food supply. You may not get to produce the volume of food that your rural friends can grow in their wide-open spaces, but you can still grow a respectable amount of nutritious and tasty vegetables–and add to your growing sense of food security by becoming an urban gardener.

SEEK THE SUN Unless you live in a tiny basement apartment, chances are good that you have some direct natural sunlight coming through the windows of your home. A few lucky city dwellers may have a backyard or rooftop access, but for most folks, you only get what your windows and balconies provide. If you have a southern exposure to your dwelling, use these south-facing balconies and rooms for your urban garden. These get the most direct sunlight each day, regardless of season. North-facing areas will be the worst

garden spot, as they remain fully shaded most of the day.

GROW UP Like cities themselves, if you cannot grow outward, then you must grow upward. There are numerous styles of hanging containers, vegetable-growing towers, and wall installations that allow you to grow food when floor space is at a premium. The inverted tomato-growing buckets do reasonably well, but using something with a larger volume of soil is better for your plants. Vine vegetables like cucumber and pole beans can be trained to grow vertically or laterally by tying them to rope, railings, or latticework.

LIGHT 'EM UP Grow lights are often employed by indoor gardeners to supplement or replace the rays of the sun. But these are not the only options for plant lighting. Mirrors can also be very helpful, by bouncing direct sunlight toward your plants. You'll see the plants respond to

the mirrors' extra light within days. The phenomenon known as phototropism can be seen as plants grow toward the light and the leaves orient themselves perpendicular to the light streaming in. Use any size mirrors to redirect the sun to your plants, but bigger is better. You can even do a downsized version of this mirror trick by placing aluminum foil under your plants to bounce light up under the leaves.

WATER WISELY City water is treated with chlorine and other chemicals to make it safe for people to drink, but it's not all that good for your plants. Although small amounts of these chemicals seem to be tolerated by most plants and vegetables, the best way to water is to collect as much rainwater as possible (if it's legal in your area) and use that to water your plants. If you must use chlorinated tap water for your vegetables, let the water sit out in an open container for a day or two to let a significant part of the chlorine evaporate.

040 TAKE IT EASY

Since limiting factors like light and soil depth have such an important impact on urban gardening, you'll want to select the easiest plants to grow. In general, skip tall-growing vegetables, like corn, and ones with trailing vines, like pumpkin. Focus on herbs, tough perennials, root crops, and salad plants for the best results in your urban Eden. Here are a few ideas:

CILANTRO, CHIVES, BASIL, AND PARSLEY need to be replanted each year

ROSEMARY, MINT, THYME, AND SAGE are perennials that last years in the same pot

POTATOES, BEETS, AND RADISHES do better in cool conditions

SWEET POTATOES are ideal for very warm areas

LETTUCE AND SPINACH can handle short day length or low light

CUCUMBERS AND CHERRY TOMATOES do well if they have enough space and light

GREEN BEANS AND PEPPERS can handle heat and dry conditions

PEAS AND KALE can handle very cold weather

041 BUILD A FOOD WALL

If your space to grow is limited, or you just want to maximize your production, a shoe organizer and some potting soil can be used as an improvised growing wall for crops like herbs, lettuce, spinach, and small root vegetables like radishes.

STEP 1 Securely attach a plastic or nylon shoe organizer to a strip of wood or wood frame, using screws or nails depending on the surface behind the growing wall. Mount this to the sunny wall of a patio or balcony. Other outdoor installation sites can include an exterior wall of your home or a fence. Indoor installations can work as well, but protect your floors--you'll need a container underneath the grow wall to catch any water that drips through.

STEP 2 Fill each pocket of the shoe organizer with potting soil. This can include time-release fertilizer, or you can mix in your own blend. If you may not be able to water the growing wall daily, you can add water-absorbing crystals to the potting mix. These soak up water and then release it slowly, keeping the plants healthier if you miss a day of watering.

STEP 3 Plant your seeds or seedlings in each pocket and water thoroughly. If the pockets are clear plastic or vinyl, the dark soil may heat up too much in strong sunlight or hot summer months. Hang a bit of light-color cloth on each row to prevent overheating. In cool weather, however, this solar heat gain will help your plants grow.

STEP 4 Fertilize, harvest, and replant as needed. The potting soil, if fertilized every other month, should last for several growing seasons. Loose-leaf lettuce and spinach could be ready to harvest within 30 days of planting seedlings or 45 days from planting seeds. Cut the fully grown crops and replant the shoe pockets immediately for the fastest turnaround.

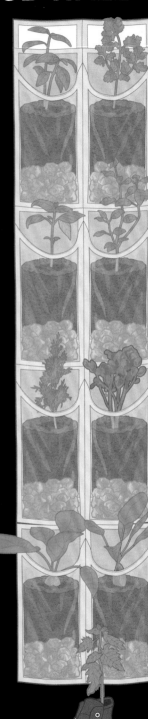

042 BUILD A RAISED BED GARDEN

A raised bed garden can provide you with a surprising amount of food from a very small space, and it works in a variety of climates. This type of versatile garden bed can tackle a number of common problems in gardening, as it can make for good drainage in rainy climates and warmer roots in cold climates. Here's how you can set up a 32-square-foot (10-square-meter) raised bed garden.

GO SHOPPING Your local home-improvement store should have everything you need, but you may already have some of these things at home, too. Grab a deer fence and assemble the following supplies:

YOU'LL NEED

6	2×8×8 boards, 2×8 inches (5×20 cm) and 8 feet (2.5 m) long
	Handsaw
1	small box of 16 penny nails (labeled 16d) or 3-inch (8-cm) deck screws

	Shovel
	Chicken wire
30	square feet (9 sq m) of garden soil (usually 15 bags)
	Seeds or seedlings for high-calorie crops

PICK A SPOT TO BUILD Pick a site with at least eight hours of uninterrupted direct sunlight per day. Less than that will greatly reduce your production. To build your frames, cut one of your boards in half crosswise. Nail or screw the ends of your short pieces to two long boards to create a rectangle. Repeat with the second set of boards and stack them for height. Align the long axis on a north-south line so that sunlight hits both sides.

DIG THE SOD Make marks on the ground that match the dimensions of your frame, and remove any grass, weeds, and roots. You'll need to dig 3-4 inches (8-10 cm) down to get most of the roots Use the debris in your compost pile.

FILL IN YOUR GARDEN BED Place your wooden frame over some chicken wire to keep pests from burrowing on the prepared ground. Fill the frame with garden soil, then plant seedlings or seeds. Water the bed deeply every couple of days.

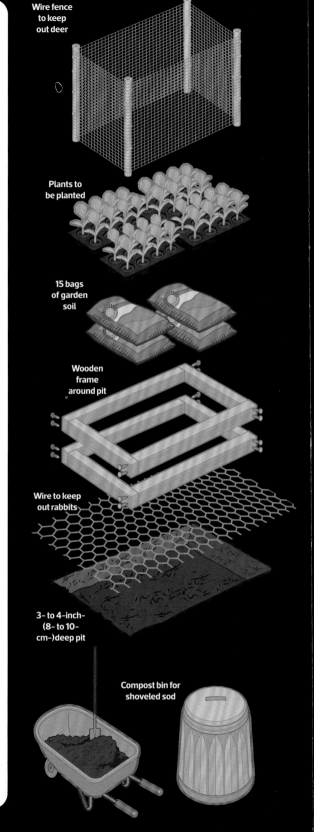

Wire fence to keep out deer

Plants to be planted

15 bags of garden soil

Wooden frame around pit

Wire to keep out rabbits

3- to 4-inch- (8- to 10- cm-)deep pit

Compost bin for shoveled sod

043 MAKE A SELF-WATERING CONTAINER GARDEN

Containers are a great way to grow food in small spaces or add extra growing space in and around your home and property. Many vegetables grow well in containers (see item 049 for a few ideas). It's best to use a self-watering container–this reduces your labor and also allows plants to suck up the water they need through their roots, which can help to eliminate any over- or underwatering. Daily watering can be annoying, and commercial self-watering containers can be pricey. Here's how to make your own with some simple-to-obtain supplies. You'll need two 5-gallon (19-l) food containers, an 8-ounce (225-g) plastic deli container of the sort you'd buy potato salad in, a length of plastic pipe, and a power drill.

STEP 1 Drill some small holes all the way around the deli container, spaced about an inch (2.5 cm) apart.

STEP 2 Using a 3-inch (8-cm) hole saw, make a hole in the bottom of one of your large containers, and then follow up with smaller drainage holes all around the central hole. Then, using a 1¼-inch (3-cm) hole saw, drill a water hole for the pipe to run through.

STEP 3 Assemble the container, placing the plastic deli container in the bottom tub (the one without the holes) and the drilled-out tub on top of it.

STEP 4 Determine where the inner container's bottom is (holding the whole container up to a strong light should make this apparent). Drill a small overflow hole about ¼ inch (0.6 cm) below the inner tub's bottom.

STEP 5 Run the watering pipe down through the 1¼-inch (3-cm) hole.

STEP 6 Fill the container with potting soil (it will fill the deli container as well) and plant your produce.

STEP 7 Pour water down the pipe until it flows out the drainage hole. This will now water your plants through their roots. Every week or so, pour a little water down the pipe and see how your reservoir is doing.

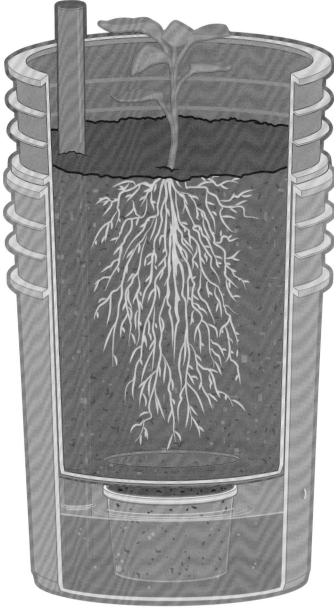

044 BREW COMPOST TEA

Here's a great way to make the most of your leafy leftovers and give your garden a nourishing drink. Obviously, this isn't the kind of tea you drink, but it's a nourishing infusion that can get your garden the minerals and nutrients it needs to flourish. Start by establishing a compost bucket in your kitchen, and throw all of your vegetable and fruit waste into it. As it gets stinky, move it to a compost pile outside.

 **STEP 1** Shovel some nicely decomposed compost into a burlap sack. The more "mature" your compost is, the better this will work, so turn your pile frequently to let everything rot nicely.

 **STEP 2** Gather up the sack and tie it off securely, then affix it to a nice sturdy stick or dowel.

 **STEP 3** Steep your "tea bag" in a bucket of water, stirring frequently, until the water is a rich brownish color. This means the nutrients from the compost have enriched the water.

 **STEP 4** Remove the bag and decant your tea into a watering can or spray bottle.

 **STEP 5** Use this tea when you water and watch your garden flourish!

045 DON'T FORGET TO WATER

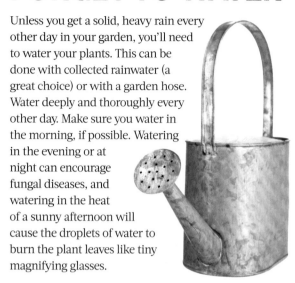

Unless you get a solid, heavy rain every other day in your garden, you'll need to water your plants. This can be done with collected rainwater (a great choice) or with a garden hose. Water deeply and thoroughly every other day. Make sure you water in the morning, if possible. Watering in the evening or at night can encourage fungal diseases, and watering in the heat of a sunny afternoon will cause the droplets of water to burn the plant leaves like tiny magnifying glasses.

046 HONOR THE AMENDMENTS

Well-decomposed compost is always welcome in the garden. The good stuff will be aged, very dark brown or black in color, and will have gone through a high-heat stage of decomposition to kill diseases and weed seeds. Add all you can to your garden, blending it with the soil or applying on the surface as a "top dressing." You can also add sand to clay-filled soil, add clay to sandy soil, or add aged manure to any soil at all.

047 SPROUT SOME SPROUTS

Do you miss gardening in the dead of winter? One of the simplest food plants to grow is sprouts! Alfalfa and mung beans are popular choices for home sprouting, but I'm also fond of radish, mustard, and broccoli sprouts. You can also use lentils, soy beans, beets, peas, and sunflower seeds, among many others. This can be a fun activity for all ages, and it's a great introduction to home gardening.

Get started by purchasing some seeds for sprouting (many companies sell sprouting mixes, and these usually cost less than small seed packets intended for gardening). Pick out a clean glass jar, ideally a clear one so the sprouts can get light on the last day or two of growing. You'll also need a lid of sorts. Mesh lids are available in some sprouting kits, though a bit of course cloth and a rubber band will do. These allow airflow into the jar and act as a strainer when rinsing the sprouts. With your supplies gathered, add one or two tablespoons of seeds in the jar and cover the seeds with a few inches of clean water.

Allow them to soak overnight, drain away the water, rinse the seeds with fresh water, and drain again. Rinse and drain your seeds at least twice a day, preventing them from drying out. Large seeds grow quickly, only taking a day or two to harvest. Smaller seeds may need several days to grow to a harvestable size. Just make sure they don't dry out in the jar. Place the jar in a sunny window on the final day before use to green them up (if desired). Store in the refrigerator and use within a few days.

048 RAISE HERBS AT HOME

An herb garden can provide some great additions to your meals, and it doesn't need to take up much room. In warmer climates, you might be able to grow herbs year round.

SAGE The fresh or dried leaves of this plant are a tasty addition to holiday meals and in poultry and pork dishes. Common sage (also called garden sage) bears a strong flavor and grows well in a wide range of conditions. In milder growing zones, it can be grown as a perennial, though it's treated as an annual in colder zones.

MINT This aromatic perennial herb is good in desserts, Thai, and Vietnamese dishes. The fresh or dried leaves can also be brewed into tea (see recipe, #39). Mint is easy to grow, but keep it contained as it can become invasive).

OREGANO Tough little oregano plants can grow almost anywhere, but they prefer warm, sunny locations and lighter soils. The leaves are a classic flavor in Italian dishes. A hardy perennial herb, the leaves work well fresh or dried. It's believed to be an antiviral herb, so eat up during cold and flu season.

BASIL This annual plant will need to be replanted each year, unless it reseeds itself naturally. Basil varieties vary, but the leaves are excellent added to sauces, either fresh or dried. To stimulate more leaf growth and encourage a bushier plant, pinch the tops from the plants as you harvest them.

THYME The tiny leaves of thyme pack a large amount of flavor, working well in sausage, sauces, gravies, and pork dishes. While thyme plants are technically perennials, they are short-lived and sometimes killed by harsh winter weather (leading some to treat them like annuals). Grow your thyme in a protected spot for year-round endurance.

049 GROW THE RIGHT VEGGIES

When you have limited space for your survival garden, you want to get the most nutritional bang for your buck. The numbers next to each vegetable reflect a ranking system created by the Center for Science in the Public Interest. This ranks different vegetables (with kale at the top) according to multiple nutritional ratings as well as their vitamins, minerals, and nutrients. The labels also note which plants do well in containers vs. raised beds, which are particularly cold- or heat-resistant, and which are the easiest to grow for beginners.

931 SPINACH ●●●

464 RADICCHIO ●●●

570 PUMPKINS ●●●

700 SWISS CHARD ●●●●●

152 BOK CHOY ●●●

420 BROCCOLI ●●

CHOOSE YOUR VEGGIES

● VERY EASY TO GROW
● GREAT FOR CONTAINERS
● GREAT FOR RAISED BEDS
● GOOD IN COLD TEMPS
● GOOD IN HOT TEMPS

NUTRITIONAL RANKING NUMBER

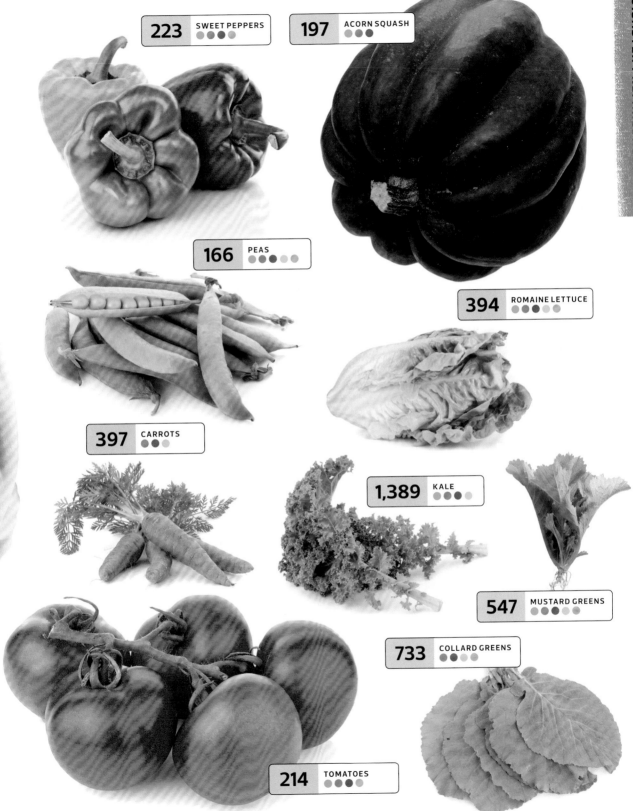

223 SWEET PEPPERS ●●●●○

197 ACORN SQUASH ●●●○○

166 PEAS ●●●○○○

394 ROMAINE LETTUCE ●●●●●○

397 CARROTS ●●●○○

1,389 KALE ●●●○○

547 MUSTARD GREENS ●●●●○

733 COLLARD GREENS ●●●○○

214 TOMATOES ●●●○○

ITALIAN FROZEN VEGETABLE BLEND

MAKES 4 BAGS (3 SERVINGS EACH)

When it comes to the conveniences of the modern kitchen, frozen food is right up at the top of my list. Through the magic of a subfreezing household appliance, we can store food for months (or even years) without it spoiling. These foods also keep much of their nutritional value with textures that stay closer to their raw form (when compared to canned vegetables, which are mushy because the canning process essentially boils them). I'm not shy about my use of frozen vegetables. Sure, fresh veggies are outstanding, but they also spoil quickly (sometimes before you get a chance to use them). That's why I have many different frozen vegetables in my freezer, and I use them nearly every day in my kitchen. So when you need a quick vegetable addition to a soup or an extra side dish, reach for the freezer handle and see what cryogenically preserved treasures are waiting inside (like this versatile Italian vegetable blend).

- ½ cup (1 stick) (113 g) butter, softened
- ½ teaspoon (2.5 g) Italian Seasoning (see item #011)
- ¼ teaspoon (1 g) salt
- 1 clove garlic, minced
- 2 ears corn, husks and silks removed
- 2 cups broccoli florets
- 3 medium carrots, bias-sliced ¼ inch (6 mm) thick
- 1½ cups (190 g) zucchini, bias-sliced ½ inch (1.2 cm) thick
- 1 large red or yellow sweet pepper, cut into bite-size strips
- 1 small sweet onion, cut into thin wedges

1. In a medium bowl stir together butter, Italian Seasoning, salt, and garlic. Shape butter mixture into a 5-inch (12.5-cm) log. Wrap in waxed paper or plastic wrap. Freeze for 1 hour or until firm. Cut butter into eight slices. Place in a freezer container and freeze until needed.

2. Meanwhile, in a large pot cook corn, covered, in enough boiling water to cover for 1 minute. Add broccoli, carrots, and zucchini. Cook, covered, for 2 minutes; drain. Plunge vegetables into an extra-large bowl filled with ice water until cooled completely. Use a sharp knife to cut kernels from cobs (do not scrape). Transfer the remaining vegetables to a paper towel-lined tray and pat dry.

3. Line a 15x10-inch (38x26-cm) rimmed baking pan with parchment paper. Spread corn kernels, drained vegetables, sweet pepper, and onion in an even layer in the prepared pan. Freeze, loosely covered, until almost firm, about 1 hour.

4. Divide vegetables evenly among four 1-quart (1-l) freezer bags or vacuum-seal bags. Add two slices frozen seasoned butter to each bag. Squeeze air from freezer bags or vacuum-seal. Label and freeze for up to 6 months.

5. To prepare, pour one portion frozen vegetable blend into a medium saucepan. Cook, covered, over medium heat for 5 minutes or until butter is melted and vegetables are heated through, stirring occasionally. Season to taste with salt and pepper.

050 REPURPOSE KITCHEN IMPLEMENTS

Has your oven blown a circuit? Did a power surge fry your microwave? Or did the apocalypse shut off the gas flow to your fancy commercial-kitchen-quality cooktop? It can be hard to cook foods when you haven't the "right" implement, but you might be surprised at the versatility of various kitchen gadgets when you get creative and put them to use in ways that they weren't originally intended. Little kitchen hacks are no big deal when creative cooks can open their minds. You could

certainly grind spices, powder some herbs, or turn granulated sugar into powdered sugar by using a coffee grinder (when you have the power to run the device). You could also use a gas oven as a simple dehydrator, by hanging very thin salted meat strips from the rack (the heat from the gas pilot light will dry the jerky over the course of a day or two).

But when the utilities are down, you'll have to get a little more aggressive if you're going to perform any tasks with a real impact on your situation.

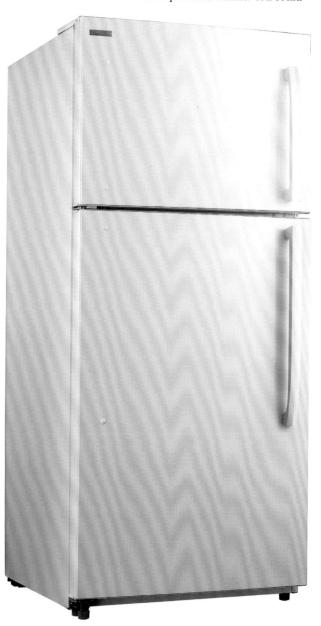

HOME ON THE RANGE If doomsday knocked out your electric range oven, put it back to work! Drag that thing out into the yard after a grid-destroying event (like a major natural disaster or an EMP attack). Toss a few shovels full of embers into the bottom of the oven, add some food onto the racks, and close the door. You just created a meat smoker! Keep adding coals to the bottom of the oven and keep the door shut. Proceed until the meat is falling off the bone.

KEEP WASHING DISHES So your dishwasher is down. There's no use crying over it. Become the dishwasher you've always needed. Pull the racks from your dishwasher and use them to dry your hand-washed dishes in the sun. Just a little soapy water, a clear-water rinse, and a few hours of UV solar bombardment will keep your dishes sparkling and prevent them from making people sick with bacterial illness. It may seem goofy, but being an effective dishwasher can save people from major health risks in an emergency setting (and plenty of other situations).

MAKE A FRIDGE SAFE If the power is gone, your electric refrigerator may seem like a waste of space. It might be, but not if you have food and other items you'd like to protect. A powerless fridge still has usefulness, by protecting things from mice and insect pests (if the door seals are tight). Now motivated mice may chew through the soft flexible seals if they can smell food inside. Pests like roaches and other troublemakers, however, probably won't get through. A fridge can also protect items from moisture. Leave it standing upright to take advantage of the shelves. Flip it onto it's back to make it into a large tool chest.

051 FERMENT YOUR FOODSTUFFS

In addition to fermenting alcohol (see item 152), this organic process can create plenty of other things to eat and drink (yes, there's more to fermentation than making bread or beer). Today we tend to focus on fermenting to produce interesting flavors. To our ancestors, however, fermentation was a way to preserve foods for storage. For example, a raw head of cabbage would quickly mold when stored "as is" fresh from the field. But by crushing the chopped leaves with the right kind of salt, microbes can break down certain substances in the food and create new ones (process called lacto-fermentation). This happens when the beneficial bacteria

Lactobacillus (which is present on the cabbage naturally) converts sugars in the cabbage into lactic acid, which acts as a natural preservative by inhibiting the proliferation of dangerous bacteria. In exchange for this homey place to live (the kraut crock), this fermentation organism provides us with beneficial live cultures that can rebalance our gut flora (like yogurt), and it can provide essential nutrients as well. There are a lot of fermented foods out there, so don't be shy about working your way through a list. From buttermilk and kombucha, to yogurt and kimchi, fermented foods are both flavorful and healthy.

052 SAVOR SAUERKRAUT

Cabbage is one of the most popular fermented vegetables in the world, often transformed into sauerkraut and kimchi. Sure, fermenting can smell pretty rank a few days into the process, but just wait–it will soon smell "right." Cabbage naturally has the organisms on it to ferment, and these steps are all it takes.

STEP 1 Get a glazed crock or a large glass jar to use as your fermenting vessel, and pick up a package of salt without iodide. Natural sea salt or kosher salt are fine choices. Iodide can prevent fermentation, so regular table salt is not recommended for kraut-making or other food fermentation.

STEP 2 Chop up your cabbage into small pieces or shred it into strips. Rinse it, then drain it for 5 minutes.

STEP 3 Place enough cabbage in the vessel to cover the bottom and sprinkle on a few grams of salt. Then use a wooden spoon, potato masher, or kraut stomper to mash the salt into the cabbage leaves for one minute. Add more layers of cabbage to the vessel, along with more salt, and repeat this stomping process. Do this until the container is full or you run out of cabbage.

STEP 4 Cover the cabbage with a weight that will keep the cabbage submerged in the liquid. Allow the kraut to naturally ferment for a week or two, scooping off the scum that forms periodically, then you can start eating it. Keep the container in a cool place, such as a basement.

053 START YOUR SOURDOUGH

While it's not everyone's preferred bread, sourdough has a special flavor and unique texture that you just won't find in ordinary breads. Sourdough relatives can be found across the globe, from the classic

San Francisco sourdough loaf to Ethiopian injera (a sourdough flatbread made from the world's tiniest grain, a seed called teff). Even if this sharp taste isn't your favorite, sourdough starter can be a handy alternative to dry yeast (in case the store shelves run dry again, as they did during pandemic panic buying in 2020). Sourdough starter can also be a great long-term addition to your prepared kitchen. (In fact, some people keep theirs for years, passing their starters and recipes down through generations!) Here's how to create and maintain your own sourdough starter. Begin with 3 cups (720 ml) warm water, 1½ tablespoons (13 g) active dry yeast, 1 teaspoon (5 g) sugar, and 3 cups (400 g) all-purpose flour. Combine the water, yeast, and sugar first, making sure the yeast starts to foam. Add the flour and stir in lots of air. Let it sit in a warm, dark place for 12 hours. Use the starter one cup (240 ml) at a time, replacing it with 1 cup (240 ml) water and 1 cup (140 g) flour to maintain the original starter batch. Sourdough starter can be held for up to a week in the refrigerator or cold root cellar. It can also be smeared onto parchment and dried for long-term storage. Allow it to dry until it cracks, and store the crumbled pieces in an airtight jar in a cool, dry, dark location. Reanimate a handful of these "chips" with equal amounts of flour and water, plus a pinch of sugar.

054 GET THAT BREAD

Now that you've learned how to create your own sourdough fermentation, let's apply that information and start baking. There's nothing like the scent of fresh baked bread drifting through the kitchen, and when served hot with melting butter, this simple food can satisfy anyone. Gather together: 1 package (¼ ounce) (7 g) active dry yeast (or 1 cup (240 ml) sourdough starter mix), 2¼ cups (600 ml) warm water (110°F to 115°F), 3 tablespoons (37.5 g) sugar (plus ½ teaspoon (2.5 g) sugar for the yeast), 1 tablespoon salt (5 g), 2 tablespoons (10 ml) canola oil, and 6½ cups (880 g) bread flour. In a large bowl combine the yeast and ½ teaspoon sugar with the 2¼ cups warm water. Let it sit until the yeast starts bubbling (this is called proofing the yeast–making sure it's alive). Combine the remaining sugar with the salt and 3 cups (400 g) flour. Add the oil to the yeast mixture. Pour your wet mixture into the flour mixture and stir until smooth. Add the remaining flour, slowly and just ½ cup (70 g) at a time, until

your ingredients form dough. Knead the dough on a lightly floured surface for 10 minutes. Allow the dough to rest in a greased bowl, covered with a tea towel in a warm location. In 1½ to 2 hours, the dough should double in size. Punch it down (exactly what it sounds like), divide it in half on a floured surface, and shape each half into a loaf. Place each loaf in a greased 9×5-inch (23x13-cm) loaf pan and cover again. Let the dough rise one last time, about 1 to 1½ hours. Bake at 375°F (190°C) until golden brown (30 to 35 minutes). Cool the bread on wire racks after removing it from the pans. Enjoy while still warm or once the bread cools.

055 CREATE YOGURT FROM SCRATCH

Yogurt is another global fermented food product created by bacterial fermentation. Cow milk is widely used, but horse, water buffalo, goat, and yak milk can also be transformed into yogurt. You'll only need a few things to make it. A container, some milk, and the appropriate live cultures will give you a basic plain yogurt, to which you can add your own favorite flavors and sweeteners. Here's a very simple step-by-step recipe, using store-bought yogurt to provide the necessary live yogurt cultures. Enjoy!

STEP 1 On your next trip to the store, get 1 gallon (4-l) of milk (2% or whole, cow milk or other) and 1 cup (240 ml) of plain yogurt with active cultures. Add the milk to a cooking pot and bring it to a boil over a medium-high heat, stirring often to prevent scorching. Drop the heat to a simmer, still stirring occasionally for 10 minutes. This cooking is vital to denature the milk proteins and create a smooth yogurt.

STEP 2 Turn off the heat under the pot of milk and allow it to cool, until it's just over 100°F (38°C). Add the plain yogurt to the milk; there's no need to stir it in. Cover the pot with a tight lid, and wrap the covered pot in a few towels or a blanket to hold in the remaining heat.

STEP 3 Place the insulated pot in a warm location and leave it for at least 6 hours (though 10 hours, or even overnight, would be better). Move your yogurt into a refrigerator, and it will continue to thicken. Use within one week for best results. Save 1 cup (240 ml) of your homemade yogurt to make another batch in the future. You'll get about 16 servings of yogurt from this recipe, each serving providing more than 8 grams of protein and very little cholesterol!

056 MAKE GOAT-MILK CHEESE

Raising goats can be challenging and costly. Most people interested in goats, though, are more interested in the milk than the potential for meat. Rather than raising a herd yourself, locate a source for goat milk. Under normal circumstances, you can find goat milk in most markets. Better yet, make friends with a goat owner so you can get milk straight from the source. Here's an easy recipe for making cheese, one of the best uses for goat milk. Unlike other recipes that require a cheese base and special cultures, this approach will work anytime.

STEP 1 Heat a medium saucepan with goat milk to 180°F (82°C). It should take about 15 minutes.

STEP 2 Remove from heat and stir in ¼ cup (60 ml) fresh lemon juice. Let sit until it begins to curdle (about 20 seconds).

STEP 3 Line a colander with several sheets of cheesecloth. (Don't scrimp on the cloth.) Place the colander in a large bowl. Ladle the milk into the cheesecloth.

STEP 4 Tie the four corners of the cheesecloth around a wooden spoon, and set it over a very deep bowl.

STEP 5 Let it drain for 1 to 1½ hours until what remains in the cheesecloth is a smooth, ricotta-like mixture.

STEP 6 Transfer into a fresh bowl and add coarse salt, grated garlic, and fresh herbs. This cheese is best eaten immediately because the herbs and curds can deteriorate. If stored in an airtight container in the refrigerator it will keep for a few days.

CLASSIC DILL PICKLES

MAKES 8 PINTS

you're growing your own cucumbers on an apartment balcony or at your survival homestead, your success may bring a problem. When your plants are heavy producers, you may be left scrambling to find uses for a bumper crop of cucumbers before they spoil. These watery vegetables are not long-lasting on their own, but they can be set aside for months (or even a few years) if you know how to pickle them. Making pickles has been a summer tradition in my mother's kitchen since I was old enough to eat them. While I'm a big fan of the crunch of refrigerator pickles, nothing takes me back like an old-fashioned dill pickle. Create your own summertime institution by learning this simple pickle recipe and the process of "water bath" canning.

pounds (2 kg) (4-inch) (10 cm) pickling cucumbers (about 48)

cups (1 l) water

cups (1 l) white vinegar

⅓ cup (100 g) pickling salt

⅓ cup (70 g) sugar

heads fresh dill or 8 tablespoons (61 g) dill seeds

teaspoons (20 g) assorted color or black peppercorns

cloves garlic, peeled and halved

teaspoons (24 g) mustard seeds

1. Wash eight pint jars and lids with hot, soapy water. Rinse well and place on a clean towel, open sides up, to dry. (Set screw bands aside.) Place the jars in a boiling-water canner and cover with hot water. Bring to a boil over medium heat and simmer for 10 minutes. Place lids in a small saucepan and cover with hot water. Bring to a boil over medium heat and simmer for 10 minutes. Keep the jars and lids submerged in hot water, covered, until ready to use.

2. Rinse cucumbers thoroughly with cold water; drain. Remove stems and cut off a slice from the blossom ends. In a large stainless-steel or enamel pan stir together the 4 cups (1-l) water, the vinegar, salt, and sugar. Bring to boiling, stirring to dissolve sugar.

3. To each jar, add 1 head dill (or 1 tablespoon (7.5 g) dill seeds), 1 teaspoon (2.5 g) peppercorns, 2 garlic clove halves, and 1 teaspoon (3 g) mustard seeds. Pack cucumbers into the jars; trim ends if they stand higher than ½ inch (1.2 cm) below top of the jar. Pour the hot vinegar mixture over cucumbers, to within ½ inch of the top. Wipe jars and tighten lids just to fingertip tight.

4. Place filled jars on the canning rack and lower into the water. Place lid on the canner and bring to boiling. Process for 5 minutes (start timing when water boils). Remove jars and transfer to wire racks to cool for 12 to 24 hours.

5. Press the center of each lid to check that it's concave. Remove screw band and try to lift off lid with your fingertips; if you can't, it has a good seal. Replace screw band. Place any jars that haven't sealed properly in the refrigerator and use them first. Let jars stand at room temperature at least 2 weeks before using to develop flavor.

057 MAKE A CANNING KIT

You don't need much equipment for canning. All you really need are jars, a large pot, and a way to get your jars out of the boiling water. Start by buying a few items at a time until you have everything assembled.

CANNING JARS, METAL RINGS, AND NEW LIDS These are essential supplies for canning. Make sure you use canning-jar lids, as the undercoating is designed to resist the corrosion from the high-acid foods inside. Always use new lids when you're canning, as the rubber seal is what allows the lid to stick to the jar, and you want to make sure the undercoating is strong.

DEEP POT Remember those old-school enamelware pots—those blue or black ones with the white dots? That's the kind you're after. You can find them in most hardware stores or kitchen outlets. Make sure the pot comes with a canning rack that fits inside the base of

go with enamelware (or you're not canning very much), you can also use a 9-quart (8.5-l) stockpot.

8-QUART (7.5-L) PRESERVING PAN This will take care of most of your cooking. You want a wide pan so that jams and preserves can boil off liquids in a hurry.

WOODEN SPOON This is an essential item for every kitchen, whether you're canning or not. When canning preserves, you'll use the handle to remove air bubbles inside the jar.

MISCELLANEOUS OPTIONS Some optional elements that will make your canning easier include a scale for precise measuring of ingredients, a measuring cup or ladle, a large funnel to help fill your jars easily, a jar lifter (you can DIY one with rubber bands around metal tongs, but you'll be happier with a specifically designed tool), and a candy thorm

058 CAN IN A WATER BATH

You should be canning by season to have year-round access to the fruits (and vegetables) of your labor. Water-bath canning is far and away the most common form of home-preserving food stores. Fortunately, it's also easy as pie.

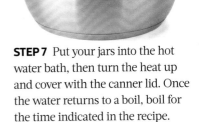

STEP 1 Fill your canning pot with water and turn the burner on high. The water will reach a boil in about 30 minutes.

STEP 2 While your water is heating, thoroughly wash your canning jars, rings, and lids, even if they're new. Put them in the canning pot and let them heat up along with the water. If a recipe calls for sterilizing a jar (just make this a habit in any case), be sure the jar, lids, and rings are submerged in a rolling boil for a full 10 minutes.

STEP 3 Use your jar-lifter to remove the lids and rings from the boiling water, and set them aside in a heatproof bowl. Leave the jars in the boiling water until ready to fill.

STEP 4 Make the preserve or pickle as called for in the recipe. You'll actually be performing this step during the time the water is boiling and your jars are sterilizing.

STEP 5 Fill your jars. To fill, pull a jar out with your lifter, empty the boiling water back into the pot, then immediately fill with preserves. Use a ladle or measuring cup to pour the contents slowly into your funnel. Make sure to pour the contents as close to the bottom of the funnel as possible to limit air bubbles.

STEP 6 After eliminating large air bubbles with your wooden spoon handle, wipe the edges clean and put the jar lids and rings on; tighten them down (but not too tightly).

STEP 7 Put your jars into the hot water bath, then turn the heat up and cover with the canner lid. Once the water returns to a boil, boil for the time indicated in the recipe.

STEP 8 Remove the jars and set them aside to cool. You'll need to leave them alone for 12 hours, undisturbed, so have a space set up out of the way for them to cool.

STEP 9 Check that all your jars have a good seal. Push down on the lid. If it doesn't move, you have a good seal. If it "pops" up and down easily, put it in the refrigerator and eat within a few days.

STRAWBERRY JAM

MAKES 7 HALF-PINTS

Few things capture the flavor and spirit of early summer like strawberries. This little red fruit is native to the New World. Wild specimens favor shady, damp areas with rich soil, but cultivated varieties can grow in many different soil types and climates. These small, sweet fruits pack a punch of aroma and taste, but they are also loaded with vitamins. Humans aren't the only creatures that adore strawberries—virtually every bug and wild creature will eat these fragrant fruits when they have a chance. Ripe strawberries are also quick to spoil, and are readily preserved by turning them into strawberry jam. Here's how to cram all the sweetness of early summer into a jar (and save it for the colder bleaker days ahead).

3   quarts (2 kg) fresh strawberries

1   1.75-ounce (50 g) package regular powdered fruit pectin

½   teaspoon (2 g) butter

7   cups (1.5 kg) sugar

1. Hot preserves go into hot sterilized jars. Wash seven half-pint jars and lids with hot, soapy water. Rinse well and place on a clean towel, open sides up, to dry. (Set screw bands aside.) Place the jars in a boiling-water canner and cover with hot water. Bring to a boil over medium heat and simmer for 10 minutes. Place lids in a small saucepan and cover with hot water. Bring to a simmer over medium heat (do not boil). Keep the jars and lids submerged in hot water, covered, until ready to use.

2. Wash, hull, and crush strawberries; you should have 5 cups (1.2 l). Place crushed berries in an 8-quart (7.5-l)heavy pot; stir in pectin and butter until pectin is dissolved. Bring the strawberry mixture to a full rolling boil (a boil that can't be stirred down) over high heat, stirring constantly. Add sugar all at once. Return to boiling; boil for 1 minute, stirring constantly. Remove from the heat; skim off foam with a metal spoon.

3. Using tongs, remove one jar at a time from hot water; pour water back into pot. Using a wide-mouth funnel, ladle jam into the hot jar to within ¼ inch (6 mm)of the top. Run a knife down the side of the jar to release trapped air bubbles. Wipe the jar rim and place lids on jars; add screw bands and tighten just to fingertip tight.

4. Place filled jars on the canning rack and lower into the water. Place lid on the canner and bring to boiling. Process for 5 minutes (start timing when water boils). Remove jars and transfer to wire racks to cool for 12 to 24 hours.

5. Press the center of each lid to check that it's concave. Remove screw band and try to lift off lid with your fingertips; if you can't it has a good seal. Replace screw band. Place any jars that haven't sealed properly in the refrigerator and use them first.

Note: The jam may need to stand for 1 to 2 weeks after canning to become fully set, and will keep in a cool, dark place for 5 to 6 months.

059 FOLLOW THESE GOLDEN RULES FOR PICKLING PRODUCE

Our ancestors had preserving (and life without modern refrigeration) perfected. We've unfortunately forgotten many of their lessons. However, there are plenty of resources available to us in the pursuit of rediscovering some of those lost secrets. Almanacs and farm guides often provide tips for pickling, including recipes for specific types of produce.

PICK IT FRESH Always can fresh produce. The fruits and vegetables from the market may look great, but they're usually coated with wax, which will spoil your efforts.

KEEP IT CRISPY Cut off the blossom end of cucumbers and squashes, as they can contain an enzyme that will turn a crisp pickle to mush in the jar. For crisper pickles, spread your cucumbers out on a baking sheet and cover with canning salt. Let them sit overnight, which draws a lot of moisture out of the vegetables, then rinse and dry them before canning.

GET ACID RIGHT Control both acidity and food appearance with the right vinegar. White vinegar at 5 percent acidity is the best bet.

MIND YOUR SALT Never use iodized salt in your pickling. It clouds your brine and can adversely affect the consistency and color of your pickles. Canning or pickling salt is easy enough to find.

WAIT TO EAT After pickling foods, wait at least three weeks before eating to allow the flavors to mix and mellow.

060 JAM OR JELLY YOUR FAVORITE FRUITS

There's little difference between making pickles and making jams or jellies. The technical process is the same, with the obvious variation in the use of sugars. When canning your favorite fruits, use white granulated sugar, as it is the least likely to alter the fruit's natural flavors. If you're truly curious about the differences between jams and preserves, it's really all about the fruit. Jams use smaller bits of a fruit, whereas preserves have larger chunks or whole pieces. Jellies use a gelatin base to congeal the fruit.

PICK THE RIGHT FRUIT When you're preparing your produce, make sure it's at room temperature to help more quickly and efficiently dissolve sugars. Also be sure the fruits are free of bruises or blemishes. Avoid soaking berries prior to canning to keep them from turning soft. Simply wash and dry them.

DON'T SKIMP ON SUGAR The sugar in your canning acts as a preservative against harmful microorganisms.

If a sugar-free or lower-sugar product is what you're after, find a recipe to account for that at the outset.

GIVE THEM A BATH Water-bath canning is fine for jams and jellies. You can also freeze uncooked products in canning jars or airtight plastic containers. Freezer-stored preserves should be good for a year, and will last a month or more if refrigerated. If making preserves from frozen stock, simply defrost thoroughly before following your normal canning procedure.

When it comes to canning, acid is your friend. Forget reflux. You're out to prevent botulism, which is a very serious and sometimes deadly illness in the best of times. If you're in a survival situation, you have to be able to trust your food. The most common cause of cases of botulism in canning is eating improperly canned low-acid foods, such as plain, unpickled vegetables. Botulism is a threat because of its origin: the *Clostridium botulinum* spores, which produce neurotoxins. Boiling water will kill the bacteria itself, but it won't harm the spores. What's more, the spores are activated in oxygen-free environments–like the inside of a canning jar. Even if you've boiled, processed, and sealed those yummy green beans inside your jar, you can still be ingesting active botulism spores when you eat them.

Fortunately, the spores can't tolerate acid, so pay close attention to the pH level. For foods to be safely canned in the water-bath method, you need to achieve a pH level lower than 4.6. If you're following a recipe that calls for a specific type of vinegar, make sure that you follow the recipe–to the letter–and use the exact acidity percentage specified. In the event you are canning low-acid foods that have not been pickled, including meats, you have no choice but to use a pressure canner, which processes jars at temperatures much higher than boiling water (temps high enough not only to kill the bacteria but also to kill the spores) and removes the air from inside the cans.

CONCORD GRAPE JAM

MAKES 6 HALF-PINTS

Grape jam may seem more like a confection than a fruit preserve, but just because it's sweet doesn't mean it's a bad way to store seasonally available fruit. By turning grapes into grape jam, we not only have an iconic partner for peanut butter, we have a way to make our grape harvest last for a good, long time (even longer than turning the grapes into raisins). What does grape jam have to do with survival? How about a morale booster? Or a way to store an abundant fruit harvest? Or a valuable trade good? But you've got to know how to make it before you can start using it, and it's not as hard as you might think.

- 3 pounds (1.5 kg) Concord grapes, washed and stemmed
- 2 cups (480 ml) water
- 4 cups (575 g) sugar
- 2 tablespoons (10 ml) lemon juice

1. Hot preserves go into hot sterilized jars. Wash six half-pint jars and lids with hot, soapy water. Rinse well and place on a clean towel, open sides up, to dry. (Set screw bands aside.) Place the jars in a boiling-water canner and cover with hot water. Bring to a boil over medium heat and simmer for 10 minutes. Place lids in a small saucepan and cover with hot water. Bring to a simmer over medium heat (do not boil). Keep the jars and lids submerged in hot water, covered, until ready to use.

2. Measure 8 cups (1.2 kg) grapes and remove skins from half of them. (To remove skins, squeeze the grape until the pulp pops out.) Set skins aside. Place all of the grapes in an 8-quart (7.5-l) heavy pot. Cover and cook for 10 minutes over medium heat until very soft. Press grapes through a sieve or food mill. Discard seeds and cooked skins. Measure 3 cups (720 ml) pulp and return to pot. Stir in reserved grape skins and water. Cook, covered, over medium heat for 10 minutes. Uncover and stir in sugar and lemon juice. Bring to a full rolling boil (a boil that can't be stirred down), stirring frequently. Boil until jam sheets off a metal spoon, 15 to 20 minutes. Remove from the heat; skim off foam with a metal spoon.

3. Using tongs, remove one jar at a time from hot water; pour water back into pot. Using a wide-mouth funnel, ladle jam into the hot jar to within ¼ inch (6 mm) of the top. Run a knife down the side of the jar to release trapped air bubbles. Wipe the jar rim and place lids on jars; add screw bands and tighten just to fingertip tight. Place filled jars on the canning rack and lower into the water. Place lid on the canner and bring to boiling. Process for 5 minutes (start timing when water boils). Remove jars and transfer to wire racks to cool for 12 to 24 hours.

4. Press the center of each lid to check that it's concave. Remove screw band and try to lift off lid with your fingertips; if you can't it has a good seal. Replace screw band. Place any jars that haven't sealed properly in the refrigerator and use them first. Makes about 6 cups (1.5 l) (about 6 half-pints).

Note: The jam may need to stand for 1 to 2 weeks after canning to become fully set, and will keep in a cool, dark place for 5 to 6 months.

10 SURVIVAL USES FOR
SALT

1 NUTRITION While too much sodium in our diet can be a bad thing, raising our blood pressure and causing other health problems, we actually need salt as one of our dietary nutrients. Ordinary iodized table salt can provide us with both sodium and iodide (which has a role as a human metabolite and in thyroid function). In environments and circumstances that lead to heavy perspiration, it may become necessary to get extra salt to stay healthy. The alternative isn't pretty. If we sweat too much and drink too much plain water, we can get hyponatremia, a potentially deadly condition of low sodium in the blood.

2 WOUND CARE The phrase "salt in a wound" usually means that you've sustained insult upon injury, but it's also a clue about an ancient medicinal application. Yes, salt in a wound hurts (badly), but it also discourages bacteria. Any edible salt will work, though it may be too painful to endure dry salt in lacerations. For a less excruciating alternative (and a great way to remove debris), create a saline wound-irrigation solution by adding a pinch of salt to a 12-ounce (354-ml) disposable water bottle. Shake it to dissolve, pierce a hole in the cap, and squeeze the bottle to squirt water through the hole in the cap to flush the wound.

3 PAYMENT Even though salt is free for the asking at any drive-thru window today, salt was a more valuable commodity throughout much of history. At the height of the Roman Empire (and through most of the Middle Ages), salt was so valuable that some dubbed it "white gold." In fact, in certain parts of history, salt was worth its weight in gold! This recognizable value led to Roman soldiers being occasionally paid in salt instead of coin. This payment was known as "salarium" (since "sal" means salt in Latin). These Latin roots show up in the French term "salaire," which became the word "salary," which we still use today.

4 HIDE TANNING For those working animal hides into leather and fur, salt can be a very useful substance to prevent decay and dry the hides more quickly. Salt naturally pulls out moisture and prevents bacterial growth (which could weaken the hide). Simply scrape the visible meat and fat from a fresh hide, and sprinkle some salt across the damp surface. Wipe the salt into the skin briskly and you'll help shorten the drying time. Keep these salted hides is the driest place you have, and check them often for pests and damage. Salted hides tend to repel certain hide-eating insects, but not all bugs. Salt may even attract gnawing pests, like mice.

5 TOOTHPASTE Brushing your teeth may not seem like a survival priority in a short-term crisis, and it's not. In a long drawn-out disaster, however, dental hygiene can prevent a lot of woe and suffering. Salt may not jump into your mind as a normal and logical toothpaste alternative, but we have a long history of using salt for teeth cleaning. Stretching back to medieval times, a little coarse salt and crushed leaf from a germ-killing herb (like sage) have been used (with your dirty finger as the brush!) to scrub teeth clean and improve breath. Today, we'd recommend a clean finger (or a toothbrush) when you give it a try.

6 CLEANING Want to scrub the rust from your tools? Make a paste from salt and lemon juice (which creates a weak hydrochloric acid), and aggressively scrub this paste on the rusty spots with a dry cloth. You can also use a paste of salt and ordinary water to scrub cast-iron pots and pans after cooking (though don't scrub too hard, you'll take off the "seasoned" layer of burnt oils). This salt-paste cleanser is a great choice for arid regions, since it only uses a fraction of the water that normal dishwashing wastes. You can even use salt to clean your filthy skin! The same simple paste of salt and water for cookware will exfoliate human skin.

7 **ELECTROLYTES** As previously mentioned, hyponatremia is a medical condition often caused by drinking too much plain water and sweating heavily. This disrupts the balance of sodium in your blood and body. While it can occur due to certain medical issues and medications, it can plunge a healthy person into a life-threatening situation (only making things worse in a scary scenario, like being lost in the desert). Hyponatremia can present with nausea, and sometimes with muscle cramps and headaches. It can even lead to seizures, but can be prevented by adding a pinch of salt into every jug of water you drink.

8 **FOOD PRESERVATION** This is my favorite use of salt. The main reason salt was worth its weight in gold in former times, and the reason people would die trying to find it, was that salt could preserve food for storage. This may not seem like a big deal today, but imagine a life without refrigeration, freezing, canning, and all the other modern methods of food preservation. Without salt, many valuable foods (like meat and fish) just won't last. Today, we can use a saltwater solution to make preserved vegetables (like fermented pickles and sauerkraut). We can also use it to make jerky, dried fish, and many other tasty and long-lasting foods.

9 **NOSE AND THROAT** In the same way that salt can prevent bacteria growth in our food, on our animal hides, and in our wounds, salt can also help with issues of the nose and throat. If you've invested in a neti pot, dissolve a little salt in the water and flush out your nose. This salty water rinses out congested or dust-filled nasal passages and offers moisture to them when the conditions are dry (either in the winter or in a dessert). I'm also a big fan of a saltwater gargle for sore throats and mouth wounds (such as canker sores). Just shake some salt into a cup of warm water and gargle as much as you like. Relief should be immediate.

10 **SALTING THE EARTH** We've saved the most extreme use of salt for the finale. You may have heard someone called the "salt of the earth" as a description of their manner. It's a compliment, meaning that the person may be rustic or simple, but they are also good at heart and honest. The phrase "salting the earth" is quite different. When you spread salt on the earth, it's so that nothing can ever grow there again. You'll do that for weed control on your property, and you can also do it on the land of your enemies. When you hate someone enough that you also want their future generations to starve or move away, salt the earth

062 PRESERVE UNDER PRESSURE

If you want to can unpickled vegetables, soup stocks, meats, or beans, you must use a pressure canner. Of all the rules of canning, this one is nonnegotiable.

STEP 1 Make sure the jar rack is in the bottom of the pressure canner, then fill the canner with water to the manufacturer's specifications. If an amount isn't specified, start with 3 inches (8 cm) of water. If the pressure canner will be working more than 40 minutes, you'll want to add even more.

STEP 2 If you're hot-packing the jars, go ahead and turn the heat on under the pressure canner. If you're cold-packing jars, don't turn the heat on yet. Cold jars can crack when you place them in hot water.

STEP 3 Fill your clean jars no fuller than ½ inch (1.3 cm) from the top, then affix the lid and ring.

STEP 4 Close and seal the lid of the pressure canner, making sure to leave the petcock open in order to vent steam. When steam begins escaping vigorously, allow it to exhaust for 10 minutes.

STEP 5 Put the weighted gauge on top of the lid or close the petcock. Follow instructions for timing once the pressure canner has reached the appropriate amount of pressure (typically 10 pounds, or 4.5 kg). If the pressure drops, turn the heat up.

STEP 6 After the prescribed duration, turn off the heat and allow to cool 5 minutes. When the

pressure gauge reads zero, remove the weighted gauge or open the petcock slowly. If it hisses, the canner is still under pressure and needs to cool another 5 minutes.

STEP 7 Open the lid of the canner slowly from the side away from your face. Use your jar lifter to remove the jars, then set aside to cool for 12 hours. Check for a proper seal at that time.

063 CAN YOUR MEAT

The ability to preserve and store your own food is a great skill set for the prepper, homesteader, or anyone else who wants to take charge of what they eat. Canning and storing meats at room temperature may be a little scary for beginners, but home canning is very similar to commercial-canning practices and, when properly done, is safe and the results are long-lasting. Canning can save you money, and it can also help you build a pantry that will turn your self-sufficient friends green with envy.

GATHER THE GEAR You'll need a pressure canner, jars, rings, lids, a jar-lifting tool, a jar funnel, some salt, and your meat. Small jars are the safest, as they reach higher temperatures in the canning process.

FILL THE JARS Use a jar-filling funnel to add your fresh meat or cooked leftovers to a clean canning jar. Add $\frac{1}{2}$ tablespoon (7–8 g) salt to 2-cup ($\frac{1}{2}$–l) jars. Add a little less than 1 tablespoon (15 g) salt to 1-quart (1–l) jars. Wipe any food from the jar rim after filling, as food particles can break the seal if stuck between the jar mouth and the lid. Pour water in the canner until it is over 2 inches (5 cm) deep, and lower the jars into the canner.

BOIL THE JARS Screw the lid onto the pressure canner, and bring it to a boil with the weight off the steam vent. Once it begins boiling, cover the steam vent with the weight and adjust your heat to maintain the pressure at the cooker's recommended poundage for meat processing: 10 pounds (4 kg) is a typical weight for meats. Process 2-cup ($\frac{1}{2}$–l) jars for up to $1\frac{1}{2}$ hours.

COOL IT DOWN Lift the jars out of the hot water with canning jar tongs, and set them on a towel on your countertop to cool.

CHECK THE SEAL After the jars have been at room temperature for several hours, check the lids to make sure they have "sucked down" and formed a vacuum. You'll typically hear each jar pop as it cools and seals. After sealing, the lids should be solid and unable to flex. If any of the jars don't seal after cooling, use the contents that day and try to determine if the lid or the jar was bad. Check the jar mouth for nicks, cracks, or other damage. If damaged or malformed, the jar should be used for other purposes.

STORE YOUR FOOD Store your canned jars of food in a cool, dry, dark place, and use within one year for best results.

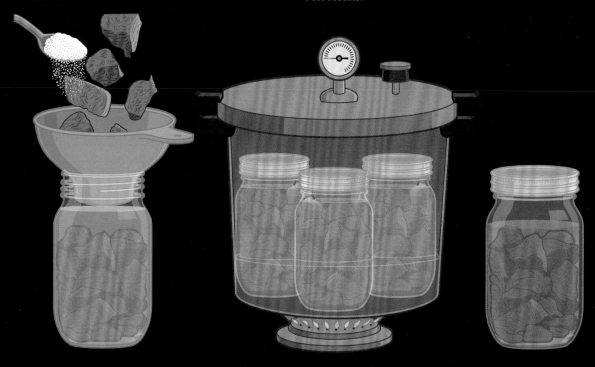

WILD PLANTS & ANIMAL FOODS

For many of us, the word "survival" conjures an image of persevering in the wild. Along with the critical necessity of shelter, you'll need to eat something out there in the wild places (which means you'll require fire, water, and some kind of raw food ingredients to transform into a meal). The food part of the equation can be the most challenging for beginners, but it doesn't have to be something terrible-tasting.

Survival cuisine can be something higher on the menu than turning over stones for bugs (unless you're into that). So far we've worked on our food storage strategies and learned how to handle home cooking in tough times. Now we'll expand your skills and confidence beyond the walls of the home. In this chapter, we'll focus on wild foods and wilderness cooking techniques. Even if you're not an outdoor living fanatic, studying outdoor cooking is an important facet of your gastronomic skill set. Learning how to perform camp cookery will add versatility to your range of survival and culinary knowledge, and it could really come in handy during an emergency. It's also a great lesson in our shared history. You really can "live off the land" like our ancestors once did and, in fact, we are the living proof that it can be done. The hunter-gatherers of the distant past were able to find enough food to survive and perpetuate our species. Sure, they likely suffered their fair share of food shortages, but they survived long enough to pass down their genetics. And even though modern people may have lost a little know-how over the millennia, we haven't lost all of the necessary skills for food procurement. We are still smart humans who are observant, patient, intuitive, and occasionally lucky. We are adaptable and creative as well. The building blocks are there, in each one of us, to become a forager and campfire cook. This chapter will fill in the blanks that you are missing, and with a little practice, you'll begin to see wild food all around you. And with a little luck, you'll never go hungry in the great outdoors.

064 STOCK YOUR CAMP KITCHEN

Unless you're sitting pretty in a well-stocked hunting cabin or a really big camp, cooking in the wild often means having limited tools at hand. That doesn't mean however, that you're relegated to cooking whole animals or making nasty food. Cooking can be a pleasure, but it can also be a job. Just like any other job, you'll do better work if you have the right tools for the job. Your choice of containers and cook surfaces are a big decision when prepping your camp kitchen. Will you need a grill, a Dutch oven, a big stock pot, a frying pan, or one of each? This will depend largely on your menu, but other factors can be involved. You'll also need something to cut your food, which could be a familiar and sturdy chef's knife,

or it could be your hunting knife (just keep in mind issues of cross-contamination if you use a bloody knife to chop raw onions to go with your cooked venison). Don't forget about the salt and spices. People on the early American Frontier were willing to risk their lives to get salt, which was necessary for seasoning, nutrition, and meat preservation. Your spice kit could be a purchased model designed for camping, already loaded with popular seasonings. It could also be something repurposed (like a small flat tackle box with small spice bottles tucked into the compartments). And life will be a whole lot easier if you have cutting boards for food prep. If you're carrying one, you might as well

carry two. These should be thin and lightweight, yet sturdy. Plastic is a fine choice, and you'll want to designate one for raw meats and reserve the other for fruits, cheese, bread and other foods that you'd cut and consume without cooking.

065 PICK A SAFE FIRE SITE

Before you kindle your fire, pick the right location, both to make the most of the fire's heat and light and for safety.

STEP AWAY Build your fire at a safe distance from any shelter–be it a hut, tent, lean-to, or shanty–a minimum of 3 yards (3 m). Take three big paces away from your shelter in the direction of the prevailing winds. Tiny sparks can easily ignite natural shelters and burn holes in tents or tarps. Also look for an area with plenty of natural wind blocks to keep the wind from blowing sparks.

DON'T BE A CAVEMAN Don't even try to build your fire under a rock overhang or in a cave. The heat could cause the rock to expand, crack, and collapse on you.

WATCH THOSE TREES Don't build a fire under any trees. Dead evergreen branches and needles are a major fire hazard. If there is snow on limbs above the fire, it will likely melt and fall directly on the fire.

PREVENT WILDFIRES Pick a spot clear of debris and leaves, or clear the ground of flammable materials at least 1 yard (1 m) away from the fire in all directions. It also pays to dig down into the soil to check for dry materials, which can start wildfires. Finally, don't build fires next to any dead stumps, fallen logs, or standing dead trees. The rotten wood may smolder for days and start a fire later.

066 FEED YOUR FIRE RIGHT, TOO

You and your fellows in the wild aren't the only ones who need to eat. If you're planning on doing any cooking, you'll need to make sure your fire is also well fed! There are three basic "foods" that your fire will eat, and it can be helpful to think of them as foods that match the "lifecycle" of your fire. Tinder is the first item on the list. It's essentially the baby food for your baby fire. When gathered in the wild, tinder should always be dead, dry, fluffy, plant-based material that can burn very easily (ideally, from just a spark). You can also prepare your tinder at home, just in case the pickings are slim or the materials are soaked during your outing. Great tinder can be made from cotton balls smeared with petroleum jelly. Dryer lint and wax soaked paper towel pieces are also popular choices to carry. Whichever tinder you choose, this is the first fuel that allows a fire to begin burning. You'll also need something slightly larger and woodier for the tinder to catch. Kindling is the second food, typically twigs, slender sticks, and very thin split wood pieces, and is needed to establish the fire. In areas with abundant kindling materials, but little larger wood, you can sustain a cooking fire or campfire with kindling only, but you'll be constantly feeding the fire. The third fuel for the fire is the bulk fuel that we typically call firewood. This may be a beautifully cut and split firewood stack. It might also be rougher material, such as large branches that you'll need to burn in half (when saws and axes aren't available. This heavier fuel will burn much longer than small materials, and it's preferred for building a bed of coals.

067 USE THIS (NOT THAT)

Fire is an element with a very pronounced duality. In one way, it's very giving. Fire provides light, heat, and safety (among many other things). But on the flip side, fire is destructive, burning anything it can. We have to be careful when feeding our fire's ravenous appetite. Just because a material burns, doesn't guarantee that it's safe or practical to burn. That's why it's important to use the right kinds of fuel in a fire–and especially when that campfire is used for cooking. The first step in choosing fuel is the selection of natural resources. You should burn branches, sticks and split chunks of wood, rather than plastic and other man-made materials. Secondly, you'll want to avoid natural woods and materials that are toxic or foul tasting. Branches, vine and wood from poison ivy, black locust, mountain laurel and other toxic species should be avoided. Thirdly, choose dead and dry wood that hasn't begun to rot. This will have higher fuel value and burn more easily than wet or rotten wood. As a fourth item, focus on hardwoods. Species like oak and beech are dense and long burning, creating long lasting embers and plenty of heat. Finally, learn about your local favorite fuels and their flavors. Famous woods like hickory, maple and mesquite can provide coveted tastes when used for smoking meats or cooking.

CEDAR-PLANK BOURBON SALMON

SERVES 4

Often associated with the native peoples of the Pacific Northwest, cooking red meats, fowl, and fish on a plank of flavorful wood has been observed for centuries (though the cooking method also shows up in Scandinavia and other locales). And whether it's a Native American original or a technique brought to the New World by colonizers, salmon is one of the most frequently prepared foods with the plank cooking technique. Salmon is such a mild flavor fish, it's like a blank canvas for culinary artists. Whether you bake it on a wood plank in the oven or next to a roaring campfire, strong seasonings can elevate this protein to another level. Our recipe blends the cooking technique of roasting food tacked onto a cedar plank with the North American flavors of salmon and maple syrup, and Old World seasonings like lemon, black pepper, and bourbon.

1	15-inch (38 cm) cedar grilling plank
2	tablespoons (30 g) coarse-grain mustard
2	tablespoons (30 ml) pure maple syrup
1	tablespoon (15 ml) bourbon
1	teaspoon (1 g) minced fresh thyme or ½ teaspoon (0.3 g) dried thyme
1	clove garlic, minced
1	tablespoon (6 g) lemon zest
½	teaspoon (2 g) salt
½	teaspoon (1 g) black pepper
1	(2-pound) (1 kg) salmon fillet with skin (1½ inches thick) (4 cm)
	Lemon wedges

1. Soak grilling plank in water for at least 1 hour before grilling. Prepare campfire for direct-heat cooking over medium-hot coals.

2. In a small bowl stir together mustard, maple syrup, bourbon, thyme, garlic, lemon zest, salt, and black pepper. Spread mixture on flesh side of salmon, and let stand at room temperature for 30 minutes.

3. Place the plank on the grill rack, and grill for 3 to 5 minutes or until the plank begins to crackle and smoke. (Make sure the rack is high enough that the plank does not catch fire.) Place the salmon on plank, skin-side down, and grill until the salmon flakes easily with a fork, 12 to 15 minutes. Let the salmon stand on the plank 5 minutes before serving. Serve with lemon wedges.

Note: Grilling times can vary depending on the thickness of the fish and the plank. Grill just until the fish flakes easily with a fork and a thermometer inserted in center reads 145°F (65°C).

Oven directions: Preheat oven to 425°F (220°C). Soak the plank and spread the mustard mixture on the salmon as directed above. Place the plank on a baking sheet; place the salmon on the plank. Bake until the salmon flakes easily with a fork, 12 to 15 minutes.

068 LAY A COOKFIRE

Unless your heat source comes with a utility bill, you're going to need a cooking fire (and there is no shortage of cookfire styles in the camping and bushcraft arena). Various campfire methods can be used to conserve fuel, which is a great option in areas where fuel is scarce. Other cookfire styles are used to maximize heat output, which is very handy when you have a large pot of water to boil. Some cookfires even use burning logs as structural supports to hold up pots and pans. This latter style, often called the hunter's fire, involves two logs of equal thickness placed close together with a small fire burning between them. While it's not as efficient as some other cookfires, a wide frying pan, grill or griddle can span the gap between the logs (almost like a bridge). By feeding this fire with small branches and split wood,

it can burn steady and stay contained. I prefer to lay the support logs in a slight V shape, rather than parallel. I also like to orient the wider part of the V into the wind, so it acts like a funnel for better airflow. Start your fire with a good amount of tinder and kindling in the narrower part of the V and you'll soon be cooking!

069 CHOOSE YOUR SPARK

You'd better be prepared when it comes to ignition sources. Sure, you could run out into the wilderness and hope to rub two sticks together to create a fire, but as anyone with experience in these matters can tell you, attempting to grind out a friction fire is no guarantee of actually making a fire. Thankfully, there are many different ways to kindle a blaze when we combine the methods of the modern world and the ancient skills and knowledge of our ancestors.

EASIEST Matches, cigarette lighters, and mini blow torches are modern marvels that make fire-starting easy, creating an open flame that can light most tinder materials on fire without a fight.

MID RANGE Old-fashioned flint-and-steel sets and modern ferrocerium rods can light finer tinder when used properly, though these sparks are less hearty than open flame ignition. Similarly, with the right tinder material (dark, flammable, and fibrous), a magnifying lens or parabolic mirror can concentrate sunlight to create an ember.

HARDEST Then there's primitive fire-starting. Nature provides us with the raw materials to accomplish the task, but these materials are not all equal, and we'll need to have a lot of skill to successfully use these methods. Friction fire can be achieved with more than a dozen different methods (rubbing two or more sticks together), though this is the most intensive group of ignition methods. Techniques like the bow drill tend to be the most user-friendly, while the fire plow is one of the hardest to achieve. With the best possible tinder (like true tinder fungus powder), we can even bang the right rocks together to create a tiny spark.

070 BAKE BREAD IN THE ASHES

When I first experimented with camp breads, I naturally turned to classic outdoor texts for recipes for bannock, damper, hardtack, and every other kind of camp bread and trail biscuits you've heard of. The recipes themselves were simple enough, but the results were usually closer to ceramic than biscuit.

Then I stumbled upon pancake mix. It turned out that the "just add water" complete pancake mix was the bread recipe I had been hoping to find. It tastes good, and it cooks very quickly! To make an ash cake, wait for a bed of coals to become ash-covered but still very hot.

STEP 1 Mix a little water with some pancake mix until it forms a dry dough ball. Pat it out as flat as you can, dusting your hands with dry pancake mix if the dough sticks to them.

STEP 2 Toss the flat cake into the bed of coals, and watch it closely as it starts to fluff up. Bake 1 to 2 minutes on one side, depending on the heat of the coals.

STEP 3 When it becomes rigid (like a little flat biscuit) and the very bottom edge begins to brown, use a stick to flip the cake over and cook it for 30 to 60 seconds more. Use a stick to move the cooked cake out of the bed of coals, wait a few seconds for it to cool, then blow on it briskly to remove any lingering ash. Top your finished ash cake with butter, jam, honey, or maple syrup if you like, or just eat it plain and enjoy.

071 ROAST ON THE COALS

The simplest way to cook something is directly on the embers of a fire. This method inevitably results in burnt food, uneven cooking, and of course, ashes on your meal. But on the flip side, it requires no materials beyond the food and fire, except maybe a handy stick to flip the food or remove it. Baking (and, to an extent, broiling and roasting) can be done directly on the coals of a campfire. I've made tolerable steaks by dropping them on a hot bed of coals, and even made better baked potatoes and sweet potatoes with this method.

GET HOT Build a big, flat bed of embers and hot ash, preferably from hardwood, before cooking. The ember bed should be several inches thick.

PUT IT IN PLACE Quick-cooking food can go in the center of the coals, where heat is highest. Foods with longer cooking times should go around the edges.

KEEP AN EYE ON IT Watch the food carefully to prevent burning, but don't turn food too often. It could end up underdone if moved too much.

ROASTED GAME BIRD WITH ROOT VEGETABLES

SERVES 4

There's an old 'possum and root vegetable recipe that you might hear about in the right hunting camp or farm kitchen. It starts with a whole cleaned opossum, and your favorite potato and carrot varieties, along with any other seasonal roots and tubers. These go into the 'possum's body cavity, as if you were stuffing a turkey. The 'possum is baked in an oven until tender, the vegetables are scooped out, the 'possum is thrown to the dogs, and you just eat the vegetables. Sorry for the not-that-funny "dad joke," but what's not a joke is the following game bird and root vegetable recipe. On this one, you'll want to eat the meat and your vegetables!

½ cup (140 g) salt

½ cup (200 g) packed brown sugar

¼ cup (50 g) peppercorns

2 lemons, halved

2 tablespoons (30 g) juniper berries or 1 sprig fresh rosemary

2 bay leaves

8 cleaned game birds, such as quail, grouse, or partridges

4 tablespoons (60 ml) olive oil, divided

Coarse salt

Cracked black pepper

2 apples, cored and quartered

2 medium turnips, trimmed and chopped

2 large carrots, trimmed and chopped

3 medium golden beets, trimmed and chopped

1. In a large pot add 10 cups (2.4 l) water, the salt, brown sugar, peppercorns, lemons, juniper berries, and bay leaves. Bring to boiling. Remove from heat and cool completely.

2. Place the game birds in a large container (make sure it will fit in your refrigerator). Pour the cooled brine over the birds. Brine in the refrigerator for 6 to 8 hours.

3. Preheat the oven to 450°F (230°C). Remove the birds from brine; thoroughly rinse all parts under cold water. Pat the birds dry with paper towels; place on a baking sheet and return to the refrigerator to let the skin dry for 20 minutes.

4. Meanwhile, in a large bowl combine the turnips, carrots, and beets; drizzle with 2 tablespoons (30 ml) of the oil, and season with salt and black pepper. Arrange in a single layer on an 11x17-inch (28x43-cm) rimmed baking pan. Roast for 20 minutes.

5. Move the vegetables to one side of the baking pan. Place the birds, breast side up, on the other of the baking pan. Coat the skin of the birds with the remaining 2 tablespoons (30 ml) oil, and lightly sprinkle with coarse salt and cracked black pepper. Divide the apple between the bird cavities. Tie the legs, if desired.

6. Roast for 20 minutes or until a thermometer inserted in a thigh reads 150°F to 155°F (66°C to 68°C) and vegetables are tender. Let stand 15 minutes before serving.

For a real wilderness feast, the green-wood grill is a great approach. This cooking method consists of a rack of fresh live sticks or branches, set up with a fire underneath. This grill acts very much like a metal cooking grill, and you may be able to get several uses out of your sticks before they begin to burn. The grill can be supported in different ways, and you can build it to any size or shape that you like. Square, rectangular, and triangular shapes are popular, ranging in size from tiny to huge. I have built several massive grills over the years, the largest of which held enough food for 70 people.

TRY A TRIPOD If you're looking for a grill with great stability, lash three crosspieces to the outside of a large tripod and then lay your greenwood rack on top of the cross members. Use vines, rawhide strips, or leather thongs to lash the crosspieces since there will be a fire nearby. Synthetic rope may melt, and natural fiber rope can burn this close to the flames. If either one yields to the fire, your rack and your food will drop into the flames.

BE A SQUARE One good adaptable method of construction involves stakes or small posts that are driven into the ground to hold the rack. Cut four stakes, 1 yard (1 m) long, each with a side branch at the end. Carve a point on the end that doesn't fork, and drive these into the ground about 8 inches (20 cm). Set two stout green-wood poles in the forks, and lay a rack of green sticks perpendicular to the poles. Maintain a nice bed of coals and low flames to grill your meats and vegetables to perfection. I love roasting sweet corn this way, just as people have done here in America for centuries.

DIG A TRENCH For another option, dig a trench in the ground and lay green sticks across it. Orient the trench in the same direction as the wind, and build a fire in the bottom. This can cook your food or support a pot of water to boil. You may even be able to skip the digging, if you can find a rock crevice or narrow ditch that already exists.

073 SET UP SPITS AND SKEWERS

There's something so satisfying about the process of skewering wild game meat on a wooden spit and watching it roast over a fire. But delicious doesn't happen by accident. Be sure you're using a nontoxic wood, and follow these instructions to produce tender shish kebabs and juicy roasts.

STICK WITH A SKEWER If you've roasted a marshmallow over a campfire, then you've used a skewer. This pointy stick offers a number of cooking options. For quick-cooking foods, impale the food on the sharp end and hold the skewer over the flames. For something that takes longer, set up the skewer like a dingle stick (see item 074), or prop it against a hearth rock.

STAB IT ON A SPIT You can cook bigger food items by roasting them on a wood or metal spit. If the food isn't easy to balance (like a chicken or an odd-shaped roast), make a spit with a side spike or barb of some kind to stabilize food as the spit turns.

barb

flat rock

074 PUT IT ON A STICK

Whether you are in a survival setting or just camping out with the family, you'll need a simple way to suspend your cookware over the fire to boil your water and cook your food. The dingle stick is one of the fastest rigs you can build. I can't even begin to count how many meals I've cooked using one.

STEADY ON While this is the least steady setup for holding a pot, it's secure enough when you build it right and don't overload it.

BUILD IT RIGHT Collect a straight stick, about 3 feet (1 m) long. Carve a point on the thicker end, and cut a small notch at the skinny end (or leave a natural "fork" to hold your pot handle). Stab the pointed end of the stick into the ground on an angle. Place a big stone or log under the leaning stick to prop it up. If you think you need it, place another big stone over the part of the stick in the ground to keep it from coming up out of the dirt. Hang your pot on the end, and adjust the height of the pot by moving the support rock back and forth.

HERB-RUBBED ROASTED VENISON AND POTATOES

SERVES 6

There have been some epic combinations over the years. Chocolate and peanut butter, Batman and Robin, tacos and Tuesdays—these pairs just belong together. There's another pair that have a long history of working well together, and that's deer meat and herbs. With some tasty herbs and a venison roast procured, you're ready to build one of the most ancient pairings in the book!

1	3- to 3½-pound (1.35 to 1.6 kg) venison shoulder roast
2	teaspoons (10 g) kosher salt
2	teaspoons (10 g) cracked black pepper
6	broiler onions
5	cloves garlic, crushed
3	tablespoons (45 ml) olive oil, divided
1	cup (240 ml) beef stock or broth
6	juniper berries, crushed and minced
2	tablespoons (30 g) onion soup mix
1	tablespoon (15 g) dried marjoram
1	tablespoon (15 g) ground sage
1	tablespoon (15 g) ground rosemary
1	pound (0.5 kg) fingerling potatoes
6	carrots, cut into 1 inch (2.5 cm) pieces
	Fresh chopped thyme, oregano, and/or parsley, for garnish (optional)

1. Preheat oven to 250°F (120°C). Pat roast dry with paper towels; sprinkle all sides with the salt and pepper.

2. In a large Dutch oven cook onions and garlic in 2 tablespoons (30 ml) hot oil over medium heat. Remove from the Dutch oven.

3. Add the roast to the Dutch oven; sear all on sides, 8 to 10 minutes total. Remove the roast from the Dutch oven. Add beef stock to the Dutch oven, scraping any bits from the bottom. Remove from heat. Return onions and garlic to Dutch oven.

4. In a small bowl, combine remaining 1 tablespoon (15 ml) olive oil with juniper berries, soup mix, marjoram, sage, and rosemary. Carefully rub spice mixture over venison; return roast to Dutch oven. Cover and bake for 3 hours. Arrange potatoes and carrots around roast. Bake, covered, 3 hours more.

5. Remove roast from Dutch oven and let rest for 10 minutes. Serve roast with roasted vegetables and top with fresh herbs, if desired.

IF YOUR DEER HUNT WAS UNSUCCESSFUL, TRY THIS RECIPE ON A 3-POUND BEEF ROAST INSTEAD.

075 LEARN TO ROCK BOIL

If you need to boil water or make a stew and you don't happen to have a metal, glass, or clay cooking vessel, rocks will save the day. Suitable rock-boiling containers of wood, bark, and stone can allow you to safely disinfect water and cook a meal. I have even rock boiled in a hollowed-out pumpkin!

The art of rock boiling is accomplished by heating fire-friendly rocks for about 30 to 45 minutes in your campfire. Gather these from a high, dry location to minimize the chance of getting waterlogged rocks, which could explode.

Once you've heated your rocks, brush or rinse off the ash, and place one or two rocks in your vessel full of water. Leave the rocks in the liquid until they stop hissing. Then replace them with new hot rocks. It will take several rocks just to bring 1 quart (1 liter) of water to a boil, but once it reaches boiling, fresh hot rocks will keep the liquid stewing for several minutes at a time.

REMEMBER THESE TIPS WHEN ROCK BOILING:
- Use a dozen or more egg-size to baseball-size rocks, swapping new ones in as you go.
- Brush, blow, or rinse the ash off the hot rocks before putting them in the liquid.
- Use a partially split green-wood stick as tongs to move the hot stones.

076 MAKE A HOT-ROCK STIR-FRY

Your hot rocks can help you cook up more than soup or stew to expand your dining options.

STEP 1 Heat several egg-size stones for 20 minutes in your campfire. While these stones heat up, chop some wild vegetables and game meat into small pieces.

STEP 2 Place the food in a large wooden bowl or a bark container, adding a small amount of oil or a few gobs of raw animal fat. Add a little water, too, in order to create steam for faster and more even cooking.

STEP 3 Pick a rock out of the fire with tongs, blow off any ash, and place it into the bowl of raw food. Stir the mixture slowly with a stick. The food will begin to cook from the heat of the rock. Once a cooking stone has cooled and is no longer sizzling, replace it with another hot stone from the fire.

STEP 4 Continue to stir hot stones through the food until all of the meat has changed color and is cooked through. Serve with one stone left in the bowl, to keep the food hot.

077 SET UP A ROCK FRYING PAN

Frying is a delicious way to go in primitive cooking. The crispy edges and caramelization that frying can create are mouthwatering. As a testament to the quality of this ancient cooking method, rock frying is still being used in modern times across the world.

GO ROCK HUNTING To get started on your adventure of rock cooking, you'll need a flat or concave stone about 1 inch thick. Avoid sandstone and other rough-surfaced stones that food will stick to. Also skip any stones collected near the water, and flat slabs of slate and shale–all tend to explode when heated.

BUILD YOUR PAN Once you've picked your stone, set it up securely with about 1 foot (30 cm) of clearance from the ground. If the rock is too low, you cannot maintain a decent fire underneath. Prop your rock pan on top of other rocks, or over a trench in the ground with the fire underneath.

TRY SOME STAKES One method of getting some height is to drive three green-wood stakes into the ground and set the flat rock on top. You'll want to stand up three flat stones underneath the frying rock to protect the green sticks from burning.

LEVEL UP To make sure your rock pan is level, pour a little water into the center–the water will run off the low side. Slip small stone chips under the low side to level it.

When you're ready to cook, build a big enough fire under the rock so the flames are touching the underside of the rock, or even curling up around the edges of the frying rock. Maintain a coal bed under your griddle, and feed it plenty of twigs and split sticks.

KEEP THESE POINTERS IN MIND WHEN MAKING YOUR OWN ROCK FRYING PAN:
· Maintain the flames for effective frying.
· Choose a rock with a slight depression.
· Don't get too attached to your rock frying pan; the heat will break it eventually.

RUSTIC RABBIT STEW

SERVES 4

For my fellow Lord of the Rings fans, the idea of rabbit stew will likely remind us of the iconic scene where Sam prepares a rabbit stew with herbs for his master Frodo (and the part where Sam has a potato conversation with Gollum that launched a thousand memes). Here's the part that's not fiction or fantasy: Rabbits are some of the most tender and tasty wild game animals on the planet, and they do make a truly epic stew. What follows is just one simple version of this classic dish, and whether you use farmed rabbit meat or catch a brace of conies with your bare hands, I hope you really enjoy your rabbit stew.

3	shallots, quartered
2	carrots, sliced
1	cup (100 g) sliced mushrooms
4	garlic cloves, crushed
2	tablespoons (30 ml) olive oil
1	rabbit, jointed into 8 pieces
3	tablespoons (45 ml) Dijon mustard
3	tablespoons (24 g) flour
1	tablespoon (15 g) butter
4	ounces (120 g) thick-sliced bacon, chopped
8	ounces (240 ml) dry white wine
8	ounces water
1	(14.5-ounce) (428 ml) can diced tomatoes
2	thyme sprigs
3	bay leaves
1	teaspoon (5 g) herbes de Provence
1	teaspoon (5 g) kosher salt
½	teaspoon (2.5 g) black pepper
	Crusty bread, for serving

1. Preheat oven to 400°F (205°C). In a 6-quart (5.5-l) Dutch oven cook shallots, carrots, mushrooms, and garlic in hot oil over medium-high heat just until softened, about 3 minutes. Reduce heat to medium.

2. Rub rabbit with mustard and coat with flour. Add butter to Dutch oven and heat until melted. Add rabbit and bacon. Brown rabbit on all sides, 8 to 10 minutes total. Transfer rabbit and vegetables to a large bowl.

3. Add wine, water, tomatoes, thyme, bay leaves, and herbes de Provence to the Dutch oven, scraping up browned bits on the bottom. Bring to a simmer and cook for 5 minutes. Return vegetables and rabbit to Dutch oven.

4. Bake, covered, until rabbit is tender and a thermometer inserted in a thick portion reads 160°F (70°C), about 1½ hours. Serve with crusty bread.

RABBIT MEAT IS SO TENDER, WITH SUCH A MILD FLAVOR, YOU COULD EASILY CONVINCE YOUR DINNER GUESTS THAT THEY ARE EATING CHICKEN STEW.

078 DIG A PRIMITIVE FIRE PIT

This might be the most complicated primitive cooking setup, but it's also the most versatile. The earth oven is a round fire pit connected to a trench in the ground. A stone cooking box spans the trench, and a mound of earth covers much of the box. The trench ends with a chimney, which rises up through the dirt mound to create a better draft for the fire pit. You can cook over an open fire in the pit, bake or rock fry in the stone oven, and cook over the mouth of the chimney like a stove top at home. You'll need a shovel or digging stick to excavate the pit and trench, and an assortment of rocks, but that's about all it takes to make this marvelous multiuse cooking appliance.

STEP 1 Lay out the pit and trench in the ground where you'll build the oven. The pit should be dug about 1 foot (30 cm) deep and about 2 feet (60 cm) across. The trench should connect to this hole, the same depth into the ground and about 10 inches (25 cm) wide. The length of the trench will vary, but I usually make mine about 2 feet (60 cm) long. If possible, orient the oven so prevailing winds hit the fire pit and travel down the trench.

STEP 2 Place a flat rectangular stone slab over the trench, near the edge of the fire pit, for a frying surface and the floor of the oven. Build up two side walls and a rear wall from chunks of stone, and place a large flat stone over the top for a lid.

STEP 3 Build a chimney out of stone or mud. Use the back wall of the oven box as part of the chimney to make it more stable and to conduct more heat to the oven, then bury the oven box and chimney in dirt. I'll often place three pyramidal stones around the chimney top so I can set a pot, pan, or griddle over the chimney without blocking the airflow.

STEP 4 Start a fire in the fire pit, push some coals down into the trench, then add sticks for more flames. Smoke should issue from the chimney as the oven box is heated by both the radiant heat of the fire pit and the conducted heat of the oven-box floor and rear wall. When it's hot enough, place your food in the oven, over the chimney, or in the fire pit to cook.

079 BUILD A STONE OVEN

Once built, a stone oven can be used over and over by simply building up the fire inside again. This internally fired oven is usually made of very large stones that can absorb a lot of heat, hold it, and radiate it back for some time. It works because the fire's heat builds up in the stones and then radiates back out for even, consistent cooking.

START WITH STONE Choose a large piece of a stone or several pieces to become the floor of the oven, or look for an existing flat stone in the ground for an oven base. Pick out some blocky chunks for the walls and plenty of little pieces to fill gaps. Select a flat rock to act as a door and a big rock to act as the top of the oven.

MAKE SOME MORTAR Dig some local clay or mud, and start building. Lay out your oven floor rocks, and build the walls around them. Find the best spot for each rock, and use mud mortar and little stone pieces to secure each rock and fill gaps. Lay the big rock over the top as a lid, and fit the door for a snug seal. Leave a gap in the back of the oven, just under the lid, to act as a chimney, and find a rock that plugs the hole to keep more heat inside while cooking. Don't worry if it doesn't look like a brick pizza oven. Just about any tight pile of durable rocks with a hole in the middle can be a workable oven.

FIRE IT UP Burn your fire inside the oven for at least 1½ hours; 2 hours would be better. Keep the door propped up to the side to absorb heat, and the chimney open. Once it's hot enough, quickly scoop out the embers and ash, place your food inside, and seal the door and chimney (using more mud if needed). Allow the food to bake for its typical baking time, plus a little extra–up to 1 hour. After that, the oven will have cooled enough that it's no longer baking; it's just keeping food warm. I have made tender, juicy roasts and sweet desserts in the deep woods with this type of oven.

STONE OVEN BREAD

MAKES 1 LOAF

While I firmly believe the first baked goods were baked in the coals and hot ashes of a cooking fire, the invention of the oven changed the game entirely. With a stable and uniform heat source, globs of sticky dough didn't have to be raw on one side and burnt on the other. They could bake evenly, just as we perform our baking today. Few food materials transform as dramatically (and as deliciously) as the grains that turn into bread. From hard seeds that are barely digestible, to raw flour, to gooey dough, and finally to fresh-baked goodness, bread is one of the world's most satisfying staple food items. It's also an item you can bake in a simple stone oven (like this quick-baking soda bread recipe).

4	cups (500 g) all-purpose wheat flour
4	tablespoons (60 g) granulated table sugar
1½	teaspoons (20 g) baking soda
1	tablespoon (15 g) baking powder
½	teaspoon (2.5 g) salt
½	cup (115 g) margarine, room temperature
1¼	cups (300 ml) buttermilk
1	large egg
¼	cup (60 ml) butter, melted*
¼	cup buttermilk, warmed

1. Begin firing your stone oven with small pieces of dry wood. Keep the door ajar and exposed to the heat so that it heats up as well. Keep the flames high and hot for 1½ hours. After 1 hour 15 minutes of firing, begin to make your dough.

2. While firing the oven, sift together the dry ingredients in a large bowl; add the margarine. Add 1¼ cups (300 ml) buttermilk and the egg; stir until a dough ball forms. Place the dough onto a lightly floured flat surface; knead for 1 minute.

3. In a small bowl stir together the melted butter and ¼ cup (60 ml) warm buttermilk. Brush the butter mixture over the dough. Using a sharp knife, lightly score a crisscross pattern on dough top. Scrape out the coals and most of the ashes from the oven. Place the dough in the oven.

4. Bake for 35 to 40 minutes, or until a wooden toothpick inserted near center comes out clean.

***Note:** If desired, brush additional melted butter on the loaf while baking.

IT'S BEEN SAID THAT ALL SORROWS ARE LESSENED WITH BREAD. BY LEARNING HOW TO MAKE YOUR OWN BREAD IN THE WILD, YOU CAN FEND OFF MINOR MISERIES WHEREVER YOU ARE (AS LONG AS THE FLOUR HOLDS OUT).

This elaborate cooking method is worth the trouble because it makes great-tasting food that stays hot for hours. The steam pit is a hole in the ground (or a raised mound) with hot rocks at the bottom covered with dirt or sand. You then sandwich-wrap food between two layers of green vegetation and cover with dirt and/or tarps to seal in the steam. This technique is used all over the globe, often for feasts and special occasions.

STEP 1 Start by digging a pit in the soil or collecting loose soil and sand for a mound. The pit can be any depth, width, or shape, and it can be dug in dirt, clay, or sand.

STEP 2 Collect a pile of rocks that are capable of handling a lot of heat. Make sure you have enough to fill the bottom of the pit–you can even place them in there like a puzzle to see where the stones fit best.

STEP 3 You now have a choice of leaving the stones in the pit and building the fire on top of them, or taking the rocks out of the pit and placing them in a big fire. Either way, the stones should be heated for two hours. If you heat the rocks in the pit, you must scoop the remaining wood, charcoal, coals, and ash out of the pit when the rocks are hot enough to avoid imbuing your food with an unpleasant flavor. If you heat the stones outside the pit, use a shovel or a large green-wood pole to roll or push the rocks into the pit.

STEP 4 Gather your green vegetation during the rock-firing time. Good steam-pit vegetation is green grass, seaweed, pine boughs full of green needles, or any other abundant nontoxic green plant material. To build a steam pit in winter, you'll probably have to go with pine boughs, as your choices will be limited.

STEP 5 Once the pit has nothing but hot rocks in it, apply a small amount of damp soil or sand to insulate the hot stones. Add some green vegetation, and then place your food in a single layer on top. Root vegetables and seafood are great when cooked in this manner. Wrap tender foods with large edible leaves (like burdock) to prevent them from falling apart.

STEP 6 Bury the food with your remaining vegetation. Cover it with a tarp and/or soil. Come back three or more hours later, dig up your food, and enjoy.

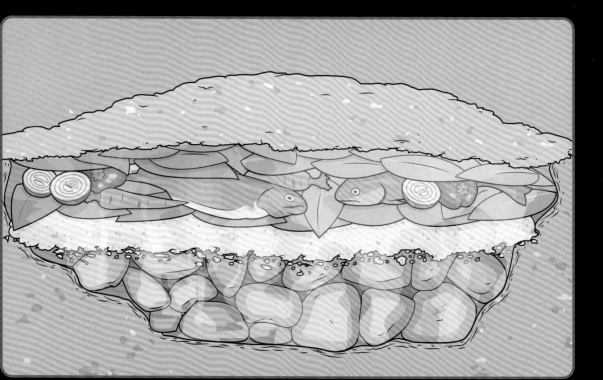

081 GET FIRED UP

You may be a master chef in your home kitchen (or even in a restaurant kitchen), but things will be quite different when you're cooking over an open fire. Without the help of all your favorite equipment and push-button temperature controls, you may think it's hopeless to try to create a gourmet meal, but that's just not true. Nature gives us everything we need to succeed, if we work within the limitations of the materials and the techniques. And these tips won't hurt at all, either.

CHOOSE YOUR WOOD Hardwoods are usually the best firewoods. A bed of hardwood coals will keep a fire burning steadily.

KEEP IT ON HAND Have your firewood gathered and ready before you start cooking, or have someone collecting wood for you so you can watch the fire and food. Split wood burns better than whole chunks. It's best to remove bark before burning (as it's not that flammable) and split your firewood into smaller sections.

KNOW THE DIFFERENCE Flames are needed to boil and fry food; coals are used to roast, bake, and broil food.

WATCH THE HEAT Food is much less likely to burn at gradually decreasing temperatures. Food is much more likely to burn at gradually or sharply increasing temperatures (so don't get impatient near the end of the cook time and stoke up the fire to a blaze; you'll burn your meal).

COOK PROPERLY Be sure you know which foods have pathogens and parasites and need to be cooked all the way through. Make sure that food is cooked in such a way to kill dangerous bacteria on the surface or mixed up in food.

082 FRY IN A PAN

Your camp frying pan can be a cast-iron beauty, your stainless-steel pan from home, or a reproduction of an old-fashioned pan meant to hang over the fire like a cook pot. Keep these tips in mind when using a fry pan in your bushcraft camp.

STAY HOT You'll need flames to effectively fry foods, so keep a pile of dry twigs or split kindling available to perk up sluggish fires.

CONTROL THE FLAME You're most likely to experience a grease fire while frying oily foods over a hot fire. Keep the heat manageable, and keep something nearby to cover a flaming pan. Never throw water or flour on a grease fire, as the results can be explosive.

BUTTER UP Greasy foods like bacon and sausage provide their own oil for the frying pan, but other foods (like eggs and pancakes) will need oil or butter to prevent sticking.

SAVOR THE FLAVOR If you've got some tasty grease in the pan (like bacon fat), leave it in there if you're planning to fry something else. Meats and vegetables are delicious when fried in bacon fat or sausage grease.

SAVE DISHES Let your pan cool a bit, and then you can eat right out of the frying pan like a plate. You'll have one less dish to wash.

CLAY-WRAPPED FISH

SERVES 1 TO 2

Clay is a wonderful resource to have in the wild (and it can even be used in the home kitchen, by procuring a block of craft-store natural clay or bringing some home from a local riverbank). When wrapped around smaller food items, the clay can seal in moisture and harden, becoming a single-use clay oven. I love to cook whole trout and other slender fish with this method, though it can be adapted to cook many foods. Clay baking is also an exercise in patience, as it can take an hour or more to cook your favorite items. It's also a great chance to practice your fire maintenance skills. That bed of coals won't maintain an even heat for an hour all by itself—those embers will need your help.

1 **large fresh trout, gutted but otherwise intact**

Several large edible leaves, such as banana, Swiss chard, cabbage, or sycamore, to enrobe fish

Wet clay or clay-rich mud to wrap the fish in a 1-inch-thick (2.5-cm) layer

1. Rinse the fish; pat dry with paper towels or a clean cloth. Place the fish on the leaves and wrap until completely covered.

2. Form the clay into a slab 1 inch (2.5 cm) thick on a flat rock, cutting board, or similar surface. Peel the clay loose and wrap it around the fish, adding extra clay to seal. Lay the clay-wrapped fish in a bed of hot hardwood coals for 40 minutes, adding more coals to maintain the heat as needed. Using a stick, turn the fish over and cook for 20 minutes more or until the juices are no longer dripping out of the cracks in the clay. Remove from the bed of coals and let cool for 2 minutes.

3. Wearing thick leather gloves, break open the hot clay. Remove and discard the leaves. Serve fish while hot.

Note: If you don't have a flat surface to press out flat clay, you can also squeeze globs of clay directly onto the fish, creating a 1-inch (2.5 cm) thick crust. Deep cracks in the clay and blackened patches on the surface are common during this cooking method. Fish is a great choice for clay-wrapped cooking, but apples are also an excellent food to bake this way. There's no need to wrap them with leaves, as they have a waterproof skin, but keep to the 1 hour of total cook time.

THIS TECHNIQUE ISN'T JUST GOOD FOR FISH. YOU CAN BAKE OTHER SMALL CREATURES (AND SMALL PIECES FROM LARGER ONES) IN CLAY AS WELL. I LOVE CHICKEN DRUMSTICKS COOKED THIS WAY!

083 COOK IN A DUTCH OVEN

These wide cast-iron pots are the most versatile cooking implements you can buy. Dutch ovens serve as a pot, griddle, and pan all in one. And they can also act like an oven, baking everything from bread to cookies. The only drawbacks may be the weight and the price, as Dutch ovens can be heavy on both counts.

BAKING To bake in the Dutch oven, build up a large bed of coals in a fire. Set the oven into the coals, and place coals on top of the lid. Try to follow the average cooking times for the food you are preparing, and replace the coals on top of the lid as they burn down.

BOILING You'll need flames underneath the oven to boil successfully. Hang the attached bail (handle) from a chain or dangle it from a tree. You can also thread a green-wood pole through the bail and support the pole with posts or convenient forks in small trees.

084 FREEZE IT RIGHT

If you have access to a freezer or you're hanging out at the South Pole, letting meat freeze can be the easiest preservation method. In cold climates, a shed can be just as cold as a freezer. To freeze, tightly wrap cut meat, and loosely wrap animal quarters or large pieces. Using wax paper or butcher's paper works well, and a vacuum food sealer works even better. Thaw it when ready, and it's like fresh meat again.

085 BUILD AN ICE CACHE

The winter air can be our nemesis if we are stuck in the cold, but it can also be used to our advantage. If you get caught without power, you can place your frozen food in a cooler full of ice and set the cooler outside in a shady area or an unheated shed. Or you can do what our ancestors did by freezing it in an outdoor ice cache.

PICK THE BEST SPOT The ideal spot for an ice cache is near your dwelling and on the north side of a large structure. This northern orientation will keep the southerly sun from warming up that spot during the day, and in the shade, your ice will last longer. Stone-age peoples made ice caches in pits dug on the north side of boulder outcroppings, to provide shade to preserve the ice and a marker to find the spot again, even in a snowy landscape.

BUILD YOUR BOX Lay out ice blocks to create a small ice platform. Your food will sit on this, rather than the bare ground. Then, using blocks of uniform thickness, build a wall around the foundation. Carve or saw the ice to make each block fit tightly. If you need something to act as "chinking" to fill any gaps, apply slush while the air is subfreezing. The slush will freeze and fill the gap. Finally, make a slab of ice that will cover the entire structure like a lid. Check the lid for fit, load in your food, and seal the lid on there.

HAVE A SECURITY PLAN Hungry scavengers will be very interested in your cache–some critters can even smell it through the ice. Most won't get to it, but for extra security, bury the ice box in slushy snow and let it freeze into a solid block. Humans with tools can break the ice and retrieve the food. If animals keep visiting the box, you could also set up traps to take advantage of the situation.

SQUIRREL POT PIE

SERVES 6 TO 8

I know, squirrels are really cute (unless they are destroying your attic and eating holes in your roof). They're also really delicious. With a very similar taste and appearance to chicken, squirrel meat can be adapted to a wide range of recipes and dishes. It can be tough, since these well-muscled tree rats spend so much of their time climbing. With the right preparation and cooking, however, the meat can be tender and tasty. Even though I'm quite fond of squirrels roasted whole over an open fire, I do really enjoy a good squirrel pot pie (and I hope you enjoy it, too).

FOR THE CRUST:

- 1½ cups (200 g) all-purpose flour
- ¼ teaspoon (1 g) salt
- ½ cup (115 g) chilled butter, cut up
- 3 tablespoons (45 ml) cold water

FOR THE TOPPING:

- 1 cup (120 g) panko bread crumbs
- 1 tablespoon (15 ml) butter, melted
- 1 teaspoon (5 g) paprika

FOR THE FILLING:

- 1 pound (0.5 kg) deboned squirrel meat
- 2 tablespoons (30 ml) vegetable oil
- 1 medium yellow onion, chopped
- 2 medium carrots, chopped
- 2 small Yukon gold potatoes, diced
- 1 cup (100 g) sliced button mushrooms
- ½ cup (75 g) peas
- ½ cup (75 g) corn kernels
- ½ teaspoon (2.5 g) salt
- ½ teaspoon (2.5 g) dried basil leaf
- ½ teaspoon (2.5 g) dried oregano
- ¼ teaspoon (0.5 g) black pepper

FOR THE CHEESE SAUCE:

- 2 tablespoons (30 g) butter
- 2 tablespoons (30 g) all-purpose flour
- 1 cup (240 g) milk
- 2 teaspoons (10 g) stone ground mustard
- ¼ teaspoon (1 g) ground nutmeg
- 2 cups (160 g) shredded white cheddar cheese

1. Make the crust: Preheat oven to 400°F (205°C). In a large bowl stir together flour and salt. Using a pastry blender, cut in butter until pieces are pea size. Sprinkle with ice water, tossing with a fork, until dough is moistened. Gather into a ball and knead gently until it holds together. Form into ball. On a lightly floured surface, slightly flatten pastry ball. Roll out into a circle 12 inches (30 cm) in diameter. Transfer pastry to a 10-inch (25-cm) pie plate. Crimp edges with a fork. Set aside.

2. Make the topping: In a small bowl stir together the panko, melted butter, and paprika. Set aside.

3. Make the filling: In a large skillet cook squirrel meat in hot oil until browned, about 5 minutes. Add onion, carrots, potatoes, mushrooms, peas, corn, salt, basil, oregano, and black pepper. Cook, stirring frequently, just until vegetables are tender, about 10 minutes. Drain squirrel and vegetables of any liquid.

4. Make the cheese sauce: In large saucepan melt butter over medium heat. Stir in flour and cook, whisking constantly, 1 minute. Slowly whisk in milk; add mustard and nutmeg. Bring to a simmer and cook, stirring frequently, until sauce is thickened. Remove from heat; stir in cheese. Stir squirrel and vegetables into sauce. Carefully pour filling into pie crust. Sprinkle with topping.

5. Bake, uncovered, until light brown and edges are bubbly, about 40 minutes. Let stand 10 minutes before serving.

086 CHOOSE WISELY

If you've never collected your own food before, it may be thrilling or frightening (or a bit of each). Some people feel like they are taking control of their sustenance and their life for the first time, while others feel like they are taking their life in their own hands. Both are true.

GUIDE YOURSELF It's an empowering thing to harvest a meal for yourself, even if it's just a tangy wild salad or a bowl of sweet berries. But you are also taking a risk every time you forage. The devil is in the details, so pay attention to the little things. Bring reading glasses or a small magnifying loupe when you go out to harvest. Bring a field guide that contains your local edible and poisonous species, with detailed descriptions. Use that book and the information it contains to stay safe.

EAT HEALTHY The time you spend can be very rewarding, as you learn to safely harvest rare and succulent edibles. And when you're in the right place at the right time, nature's bounty is open to you. Just a little bit of work (and a lot of attention to plant details) can get you an armload of edibles. Who needs vitamin tablets when you can get a wealth of vitamins and minerals from your wild meals?

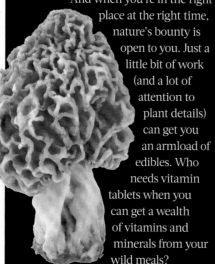

087 FORAGE SAFELY

It's important to take some basic precautions as you set out to sample local plants.

CHECK CAREFULLY The basis of plant identification is checking a plant's features against a guidebook (or your own knowledge of the species) to be sure you know what it is and whether it's edible.

One simple piece of advice: If you even have a hint of doubt that something doesn't look quite right about a plant you are sizing up, then absolutely do not eat it.

BEWARE OF ALLERGIES Wild plants aren't there just to munch upon, and some can be very dangerous to humans. You may still have an unusual reaction to a widely tolerated plant food.

088 BE A GOOD STEWARD

It's easy to think of the great outdoors as your own personal grocery store when you first take up foraging. And in the beginning, it's very easy to over-harvest–especially since everything is free. It's also easy to fixate on your own wants. If you harvested all of the edible plants in an area today, would there be more for the future?

PICK YOUR PLANTS WISELY Be a guardian to the landscape. Pay careful attention to the plants around you; your presence can benefit your local wild spaces in return. For example, when you discover an abundant delicious wild edible like garlic mustard, take all you can. This tasty weed is invasive and can choke out native plants.

RESTOCK THE REGION You can also find out which native plants are missing from an area, and collect (or purchase) edible plant seeds to spread as you hike around. You'll have a future crop, and others can use the plants, too.

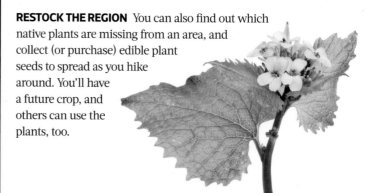

089 MAKE SURE IT'S SAFE

There are plenty of things that can go wrong when you are foraging, but you can do a lot to minimize risk by following the basic rules of identifying and harvesting wild edibles.

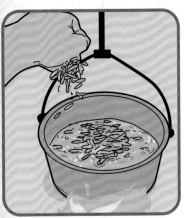

STEP 1 Use a field guide to make 100 percent positive identification of the plant or plant part (nut, berry, flower, etc.).

STEP 2 Cross-reference your research just to make sure there aren't any dangerous look-alike species.

STEP 3 Research the right way to use the plant, which parts are safe to use, and when to use them if seasonality is a factor.

STEP 4 Learn which plants should be eaten in moderation and which will require any special preparation to eat at all.

STEP 5 Reduce the risk of allergic reaction by eating only small amounts of plants that are new to you, and try just one new food per day (after you make a 100 percent positive ID).

STEP 6 Finally, if in doubt, do not eat it!

PINE BARK-OATMEAL COOKIES

MAKES 48 COOKIES

Pine bark has long been recognized as a food for desperate souls, something that only starving people would collect and eat. I'm here to challenge that notion. Yes, pine bark can be a little tedious to gather, so you're not likely to do it every day. Once you have a few cups of dried and ground inner pine bark in your pantry, it's a surprise ingredient that can leave your most adventurous foodie friends scratching their heads and wondering what exactly you put in their cookies (and by the way, cookies are the best thing you can do with pine bark flour).

1	cup (2 sticks) (225 g) butter, softened
1	cup (225 g) firmly packed brown sugar
½	cup (100 g) granulated sugar
2	eggs
1	teaspoon (15 ml) vanilla
3	cups (270 g) regular oats
1½	cups (135 g) pine bark flour (recipe, right)
1	teaspoon (15 g) baking soda
1	teaspoon (15 g) ground cinnamon
½	teaspoon (2.5 g) salt

1. Preheat oven to 375°F (190°C). In large bowl beat butter and sugars with a mixer on medium-high until creamy. Beat in eggs and vanilla until well combined. In a small bowl stir together oats, flour, baking soda, cinnamon, and salt. Add flour mixture to the butter mixture and mix well.

2. Drop dough by rounded teaspoons onto ungreased cookie sheets. Bake 8 to 9 minutes for a chewy cookie or 10 to 11 minutes for a crisp cookie. Cool on cookie sheet 1 minute. Transfer to a wire rack to cool completely.

Pine Bark Flour: From a pine tree, shave off the inner layer of bark next to the wood. (This layer is rubbery and cream colored.) Dry the bark in a 350°F (175°C) oven or over a low fire oven until brittle, about 45 minutes. Cool bark completely. Place bark in a food processor and process until a flour consistency.

Bars: Press dough into the bottom of an ungreased 9x13-inch (23x33-cm) baking pan. Bake at 375°F (190°C) until light golden brown, 25 to 30 minutes. Cool completely in pan on wire rack. Cut into bars.

Variation: Stir in 1 cup (150 g) raisins, chopped nuts, or semisweet chocolate chips with the oats and pine bark flour.

USE THE RIGHT SPECIES (WHITE PINE) AND THE RIGHT PARK OF THE BARK (THE CREAM-COLORED INNER LAYER) TO MAKE FLOUR FOR YOUR COOKIES.

090 KNOW YOUR NUTS

Tree nuts are a great source of calories when you're out in the wild, but you have to know which ones to look for and how to make them ready to eat.

ACORN Many native peoples in the northern hemisphere ate acorns as a staple food prior to agriculture. These are high-carb nuts, with some fat and a little protein. The bitter acid in them is easily removed by cracking them into pieces and soaking the acorn nut meat chunks in repeating baths of warm water, 1 hour at a time, until the bitter is gone. Don't boil them–it locks in some of the bitterness.

BEECH These tree nuts can be a valuable and delicious wild food source, but you'll have to be quick, as squirrels seem to favor them above all others. Look for the smooth-barked trees in the eastern woodlands, and keep an eye out for the small three-sided seed falling out of a prickly husk around early October.

HAZELNUT There are several species of hazelnut tree in Europe, Asia, and North America. The most common tree in the U.S. is the American hazelnut, which grows east of the Mississippi from Georgia to Maine. Hazelnuts are relatively rich in calories and are also a good source of vitamin E, thiamine, copper, and manganese.

BLACK WALNUT Black walnuts look like green tennis balls on the tree, but their rough, round husks turn to a very dark brown as they lie on the ground in autumn. The nut meats are rich-tasting and high in fat, with a fair amount of protein, magnesium, phosphorus, copper, and manganese. Wild animals might even let you get some of them, primarily because they don't like to chew through those thick, bitter husks.

HICKORY The most calorie-dense wild food in our gallery, the hickory is packed with life-sustaining fat. Most varieties taste like their most famous relative, the pecan. These sweet and fatty nut meats can be eaten right out of the shell or cooked in a number of ways. From porridge to cookies to a crust for a game bird pot pie, hickory is an underused hero in wild foods.

CHESTNUT Part of the beech family, these deciduous hardwood trees and shrubs are found throughout temperate regions of the northern hemisphere. The nut is contained in a needle-covered cupule, also known as a burr. These burrs often grow in pairs or clusters, and each burr can hold one to seven nuts. Chestnuts are less calorie-dense, but are a good source of vitamin B6, vitamin C, and potassium.

091 DON'T EAT THESE

There are at least two major species you should avoid when foraging for nuts. The first is buckeye, which, like hickory, has a "double layer" nut shell–a husk that peels off with a hard nut shell underneath. Buckeyes have a shiny brown shell underneath the outer husk, while hickories have a dull tan-colored shell. Hickory has a multiple inner shell like a walnut, while buckeye has a solid meat like an almond. Also, chestnuts should not be confused with horse chestnuts, which have similar, but poisonous, nutmeat.

092 PROCESS ACORNS PROPERLY

Acorns represent one of the biggest (and most widespread) calorie jackpots in the annual wild plant food harvest. They do require a bit of processing to be palatable, but they're well worth it.

STEP 1 Crack the shells, remove the nut meats, and break any large pieces into pea-size chunks.

STEP 2 Soak the meats in warm water to remove their bitter and irritating tannic acid. Some guides instruct us to boil acorns, but this locks in some of the bitterness. Let soak for a few hours.

STEP 3 If the soaking water was safe to drink, taste a piece of acorn to see if they're still bitter. If so, drain off the water (which should be brown like tea), add fresh warm water, and soak again for a few hours. Repeat this a few times depending on the acorns' bitterness.

STEP 4 Once the acorns taste okay (in other words, bland), let them dry out for a few hours. You can run them through a grain grinder or flour mill, or use the classic mortar and pestle to make acorn flour. Add this flour to existing recipes, or try your hand at making acorn porridge, cookies, crackers, or biscuits.

093 USE EVERYTHING BUT THE SQUEAL

Remember the brown tea-like water you poured off the first soaking of acorns? Well, don't throw it out! Even though it seems like we're brewing up some kind of medieval potion, crushed acorns and hot water can provide a great remedy for inflamed and irritated skin, as well as toothaches. You can use the first water you pour off from the process of soaking acorns for food.

You can make a concentrate by boiling crushed acorns (shells and all; a handful in one pint of water will make a small batch of strong medicinal fluid). Soak a clean cloth in it, and apply to rashes, ingrown toenails, hemorrhoids, or other inflamed skin ailments. For tooth troubles, simply swish the stuff (swallowing it causes an upset stomach).

094 DINE OFF A PINE

The nuts of any large pine tree are a classic Native American survival food, and an important food around the northern hemisphere. Pine nuts are more than half fat by weight, with some protein and carbs added in for good measure. They're also a good source of thiamine and manganese, with a decent array of other B vitamins and several minerals.

CRACK A CONE Generally speaking, the larger the pinecone, the bigger the seeds. And it usually takes some work to tear open a cone. Some species will open by the heat of a fire, but most won't; you'll have to tear them open with pliers or a multi-tool. But with a nutritional profile like this, and a great taste, it's worth the work.

MAKE BARK FLOUR Pine also has an edible layer to its bark. Shave off the rubbery cream-colored inner layer of bark that's right next to the wood. Dry the strips out until they are brittle, and grind them into flour. The flour will have a mild pine flavor and a fair number of calories. Extend your food supply by blending it with other flours.

ANIMAL FAT

1 FAT LAMPS Whether the fat is right off the animal and still warm, or you've rendered it into lard, this important resource can serve a wide range of survival uses. One of the weirdest comes when you use fat as a lighting source. Surprising but true–you can literally make a "snowball" candle out of raw animal fat. Just squeeze the raw fat into a whitish ball, insert some plant-fiber twine to act as a wick, and light it up. You'll have an almost instant fat lamp! Or for the more sophisticated survivalist, fill a fireproof vessel (like a clay or stone bowl) with rendered lard and add a wick to make a primitive grease lamp.

2 FORGE QUENCH Not everyone needs to make sharp knives and act out their blacksmith fantasies to survive. But what if you did? The ability to make knives and other tools could be an indispensable skill during the coming zombie apocalypse, or as a lucrative side hustle in normal times. Liquefied animal fat, or even cold solid lard, is a great quench "fluid" for knives and other forged objects that need hardening. The fat quench is gentler than a water quench, and pig fat was a widely used quench on the early American frontier. An animal fat quench also creates food-grade protective coating, better than many petroleum-based oils.

3 WET-WEATHER FIRE STARTER We know that fat is high in calories, but what are calories, really? It's one of the most commonly used food energy units in the world. To describe it very simply, it's something that can "burn" to produce heat. This is true when we consume digestible fats. It's also true when we light animal fat on fire! Wipe a little lard onto some tinder and light it for a wet-weather fire starter that burns with a strong heat for several minutes. You could also apply fat to wood, charcoal, or any other flammables to help them burn better and longer than those dry materials would burn without the greasy glow of the burning fat.

4 WATERPROOFING Fat and water just don't seem to get along. The fat tries to repel the water every chance it gets. This rivalry can work in our favor, however, when leather boots and other outerwear become less permeable to water with a healthy coating of animal fat. Mountain men, hunters, and trappers once wiped animal fat on their thin leather moccasins to keep them soft and somewhat waterproof when trudging through the rain, slush, and snow of the American frontier. Just smear a thick coat of animal fat over the stitching and exposed seams of leather goods, and you too can buy some time before the water comes through.

5 SOAP Chunks of animal fat have a deceptive value. When we're first learning to butcher wild game, those gross whitish blobs seem like trash–something we are trying to remove and discard from the lean meat of the animal. But a more seasoned survivor knows that those white lumps are pure gold, and in some situations–more valuable than the meat itself. One crafty use of rendered fat can be the production of soap. When the right amount of fat is blended with lye and water, then simmered and stirred until slushy, this slurry can be set aside for hardening and aging to create an effective homemade soap.

6 LUBRICANT From black powder rifles to friction fire sockets, animal fat can provide an excellent lubricant. It also inhibits rust on iron and steel objects. It shouldn't be a surprise that various animal fats have different qualities from each other, just as a fish is a very different animal from a bear. Fish oils tend to be very light and easily burned off, while mammal fat tends to be heavier and longer lasting. Using fat as a mechanical lubricant has a longstanding tradition, as the use of "mineral oil" is a more recent discovery. While you shouldn't pour it in your vehicle engine, it does serve many roles (even in the modern world).

7 **MEDICINAL SALVE** Healing plants can be combined with lard to create a wide range of salves and balms for skin care, first aid, and other applications. Dried yarrow leaves (*Achillea millefolium*) are one of my favorites when prepared with lard. This salve can help to stop minor bleeding and reduce the risk of infection on cuts, scrapes, and scratches. Simply warm up the lard to a liquid and soak crushed dried yarrow leaves in the melted oil (ideally for several days in a slow cooker pot on low heat). Strain out the leaves and reserve the hot oil. Add 1 ounce (30 ml) of beeswax per 8 ounces (240 ml) of hot oil and stir. When cooled, your salve is done.

8 **CONDITIONING** The dry cracked skin on your hands and feet can get a great healing boost from a light rub of animal fat. Your parched leather boots and gloves could benefit from a wipe of animal fat, too. And how is your hair so shiny and soft? It's not Pantene conditioner. It's a smear of bear fat. In all seriousness, fat is something that our skin and hair can crave. Similarly, the skin of other creatures (namely, leather goods) can hunger for this slippery substance, too. Bear fat (if you can get it, and the bear won't willingly give it up) is one of the best deep conditioners for leather, penetrating deeply and lasting for a long time.

9 **PEMMICAN** Fats are the densest source of calories, and every calorie can count in emergencies. If your animal fat is still "food grade" (read here: not rancid yet), use it for cooking, or simply add a little bit to other foods to enhance their low calorie content. Pemmican is a fine example of this importance for fat. This ancient forebear of the modern survival ration, pemmican was originally prepared by Native Americans as a traveling food and cold-weather snack. Traditional pemmican is a blend of dried meat pounded into a powder, then blended with warm animal fat and often supplemented with dried fruits, berries, or foods.

10 **BAIT** In frigid environments, most scavengers and carnivores will succumb to their hunger for calorie-dense animal fat, even when all their instincts are screaming, "No, don't stick your head into that scary human-scented contraption!" But when hunger drives them hard enough in the cold winter wind, they'll take the bait–when that bait is animal fat. Applied warm to trap trigger mechanisms, fat can quickly harden in frosty or subfreezing conditions. As the fat naturally hardens, this can make it harder for the animal to steal or lick away the bait without disturbing the trap trigger.

095 GO GREEN

Looking to stock up on wild greens? Here are a few great examples of edible plants to pick.

CHICORY This herbaceous perennial plant, native to Europe, is found across the hemisphere. Its leaves are similar to those of the dandelion, and the stalk has smaller alternate branching leaves. The blue composite flowers have ragged square edges to the rays. Chicory may live for several years, reviving from its taproots. The leaves and flowers can be eaten, and the roots can be baked to make a coffee substitute.

CHICKWEED This herbaceous annual plant often forms a carpet on the disturbed ground of farms, gardens, and lawns. Native to Europe, it is now found in many places. The small, ovate, simple leaves grow in an opposite branching pattern on round, green stems with white flowers. The tender leaves and stems can be eaten raw (in the case of star chickweed) or cooked (if you happen to find mouse-ear chickweed). This plant can be used as a poultice for an anti-itch remedy, and can be eaten to relieve constipation.

WOOD SORREL These are common perennial herbaceous plants in the northern hemisphere, with heart-shape leaflets in threes. Stems and leaf stalks are alternate branching, and these plants are rarely taller than 6 inches (15 cm). The flowers are yellow, pink, or purple, often with five petals. The leaves, stems, and flowers can be eaten raw in salads, or steeped in hot water, strained, sweetened, and chilled to create a lemonade substitute. Be aware: Their sour taste is caused by oxalic acid, which can lead to kidney stones. Limit yourself to occasional use.

SHEEP SORREL This small plant grows very unusual spearhead-shape simple leaves in fields and gardens. It is a perennial herbaceous plant that has a reddish alternate branching stem, up to a height of 18 inches (0.5 m). The leaves are typically small, about 1 inch (3 cm), and smooth-edged, with a pair of lobes at the base of each leaf that may point outward or down. The tender, sour leaves can be eaten raw or prepared for a drink, similar to wood sorrel. And like wood sorrel, the sour flavor comes from oxalic acid, which should be consumed in moderation to avoid the risk of kidney stones.

PLANTAIN A common weed in lawns worldwide, this annual herbaceous plant has parallel-veined, smooth-edged simple leaves that grow in a basal rosette. Torn, the leaves reveal stringy fibers inside the parallel veins and have an astringent cabbagelike odor. The small white flowers are on slender stalks, which later grow greenish seeds. The chopped young leaves can be added to salads or boiled as cooked greens. Seeds can be eaten raw or cooked and are high in B vitamins. Plantain is also a great poultice for insect stings and venomous bites.

WATERCRESS An aquatic or semiaquatic plant native to Europe and Asia, this perennial is a relative of mustards and radishes, and one of the earliest plants consumed by humans. Watercress grows in fast, clean streams and springs, with hollow floating stems and pinnately compound leaves in an alternate pattern. The small white flowers have four petals in clusters. The leaves and tender stems have a biting, spicy flavor. Just wash them thoroughly if you decide to eat them raw, as the water they grew in could bear pathogens. Cooked watercress is not as tasty, but it is safer. Watercress is a source of vitamin C and other nutrients.

096 DIG SOME ROOTS

Some plants may not be too tasty above ground, but their roots can be a great wild food source.

BURDOCK To prepare this root, just wash it, chop it, boil the root pieces for about 5 minutes, change the water, boil again for 5 minutes, and then taste-test for flavor. (Boil again if needed to remove the bitterness.) Burdock is a source of vitamin B6 and provides potassium, magnesium, and manganese.

CATTAIL Often labeled as the "supermarket of the swamp," this plants' roots contain an edible white starch, and its shoots as well as the sprouts that grow on the roots are also edible, if low in calories. The leaves can be woven into baskets and twisted into ropes. Just watch out for iris, which is poisonous and also grows in swampy conditions. Iris is generally half the height of cattail with a large flower at the top. Cattail will be topped with a seed head that looks very much like a corndog in size and shape.

JERUSALEM ARTICHOKE Neither from Jerusalem nor an artichoke, this native sunflower relative does have a slightly sweet tuber that contains lots of iron and potassium. It also provides a good dose of B vitamins. Look for the small sunflower-looking bloom in the fall at the tops of the tall plants, and dig up the tubers, which are shaped much like ginger roots.

WILD ONION Roughly a dozen different species of wild onion grow in North America. Whether closer to garlic or chives in appearance, all are part of the tasty, edible *Allium* genus. But don't just wolf down any onion-looking plant; they are part of the lily family, which contains some toxic members. Look for the classic shapes of a bulbous root and a rounded stem of onion and garlic. Next, scratch the bulb or bruise the green tops, and you should immediately smell the familiar oniony odor. If a few tears begin welling up in your eyes, all the better; you will definitely know you have an onion or garlic genus member for sure. Use these raw or cooked, just like their store-bought relatives.

097 SKIP THE FUNGUS

Sure, mushrooms can be delicious. And yes, it's like a treasure hunt to search for them in the wild. But are mushrooms a safe, reliable source of food for beginning foragers?

Of the world's 70,000 species of fungi, only about 250 species are considered to be a good wild food. Roughly the same number of species can kill you or put you on the list for a liver transplant. Everything else is somewhere in between these extremes. Most mushrooms and fungi are too bitter, too small, or too tough to eat—or are just toxic enough to make you wish you hadn't eaten them.

There are thousands of mushroom poisoning cases in the U.S. annually, and many more worldwide each year.

Remarkably, it's rare for these poisonings to be fatal, as most exposures are treatable (and happen where treatment is available), or are mild enough that no medication is required. But people can and have died, so don't risk it.

ACORN PORRIDGE

SERVES 2

Acorns are the nuts you'll find on every species of oak found worldwide (and there are hundreds of species out there, both large trees and small shrubby bushes). These common and abundant tree nuts require a little bit of special processing, but they have been a high-calorie staple crop for many of our ancestors around the northern hemisphere. Coming in at approximately 2,000 calories per pound, this is a wild food that is too valuable to ignore. Just make sure you have positively identified each and every tree nut you intend to use as food. You'll need to be able to differentiate an acorn from a buckeye, as buckeyes (and the very similar looking horse chestnut) are poisonous.

2   cups (480 ml) water

1   cup (140 g) acorn meal (recipe, right)

⅛   teaspoon (0.75 g) salt

¼   cup (60 ml) maple syrup or (60 g) brown sugar

1   tablespoon (15 g) butter (optional)

½   cup (95 g) blueberries, raspberries, or blackberries

2   tablespoons (30 g) toasted chopped pecans

       Milk or nondairy milk (optional)

1. In a medium saucepan bring the water to a boil over medium-high heat. Add acorn meal and salt; stir to combine. Reduce heat to low. Cook, covered, for 15 minutes. Remove from heat, and let stand for 10 minutes.

2. Stir maple syrup and butter (if using) into porridge. Sprinkle servings with berries and pecans. Serve with milk, if desired.

Acorn Meal: Crack the acorns out of their shell, and break any large pieces into pea-size chunks. Soak the acorn chunks in warm water for 3 hours to remove the bitter and irritating tannic acid. If the water is safe to drink, taste a piece of acorn for bitterness. If still bitter, drain the tea-color water, add fresh warm water, and soak the acorn again. Repeat soaking until acorns taste bland. Spread acorns on a rimmed baking sheet to dry, about 3 hours. Process acorns through a grain grinder, flour mill, or mortar and pestle until meal consistency (slightly more coarse than flour).

ACORNS HAVE BEEN CALLED THE "BREAD OF THE WOODS." THEIR NUTRITIONAL PROFILE IS SIMILAR TO BREAD—LOADS OF CARBS, AS WELL AS SOME FAT AND PROTEIN.

098 LEARN BERRIES INSIDE AND OUT

When we first learn about local berries and fruits, we often make some dangerous assumptions. For example, if most of our region's red fruits happen to be edible, it's easy to assume that all red fruits are safe to eat. Unfortunately, this thinking can get foragers into serious trouble. Color alone is not a safe way to judge edibility or safety. You'll need to positively determine the plant's genus and species by studying the plant's leaf patterns, branch patterns, and the innards of the fruit or berry. Before you take the first bite, check each of these seven features of fruits and berries.

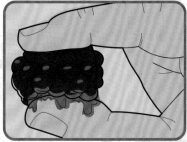

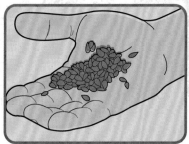
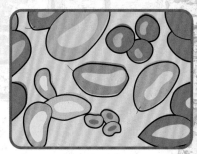

1 EXTERIOR COLOR The color of a fruit or berry is the first thing that catches our eye, and it is an important factor in identification. But it can't be your only identifier.

2 INTERIOR COLOR This can be a key difference between berries that look the same on the outside. Check carefully against your identification guide.

3 TEXTURE You may find pulp, pith, or juice when you squish open a fruit or berry. All of these are fine—provided they match what you're expecting to find.

4 SEED COLOR From pale tan to jet black, the seed color inside the fruit should be the right one for that particular species.

5 NUMBER OF SEEDS Check the seed number from several specimens and come up with an average. Some species have only one seed within, while others have many. In some cases, the difference between one and two seeds can mean the difference between an edible fruit and a very similar poisonous species.

6 SEED SIZE Check the seed size against your identification guide to make sure you have the right fruit or berry; this is an important identifier.

7 SEED SHAPE Seeds may be round, pointy, oblong, curved, flat, or any number of shapes. As with the other factors here, check closely to make a positive identification.

099 MAKE SOMETHING FROM MULBERRY

These fruits are found around the world, with black, white, and red varieties. Be sure the fruits are ripe and sweet: Eating underripe mulberries can lead to serious reactions including vomiting, diarrhea, and hallucinations. Here are some uses for the berries, and a bonus one for the bark.

MAKE WINE Mix mulberries, sugar, and water, then boil. After the mix cools and is strained into a sterile glass jug, add red wine yeast and ferment in a dark room-temperature spot for six weeks. Enjoy the new wine right away or, for best taste, bottle the wine and age for a few months.

SIP ON SYRUP Beautiful purple syrup can be made from mulberries to pour on pancakes, ice cream, or other foods. Mash 1 pint (475 ml) berries in a pot, add 2 cups (480 ml) of white sugar, and boil for 10 minutes, no water needed. Stir constantly to prevent burning. While the mix is hot, strain it into a clean jar. This is your finished syrup! Store it in the fridge for up to two months.

BAIT YOUR TRAPS Collect a few mulberries when they are abundant, and use them for trap bait where they are scarce. They will draw raccoons, opossums, and even skunks. Just don't bait under a fruiting tree; animals will never go for your bait when there are plenty of berries available.

DYE AND STAIN Black mulberries provide a reddish-purple dye or stain for wood, cloth, or leather. Mash the berries and wipe them on the object for the simplest procedure, though this tends to wash out. Boil the mashed berries in a little water with a mordant, like alum, to brighten the colors and help them stain deeper and better.

TWIST UP CORD Mulberry's inner bark is a very strong fiber, stripped from dead branches once the bark has loosened, or peeled from live branches in spring, and used as a strong rope, cord, or thread. Twist it into two- or three-ply cordage, or use it as-is for quick tying jobs.

100 BEND A BERRY BUCKET

Getting the bark skinned off the tree in one piece is typically the worst part of making a container, and for most people, it's not that bad. When it comes time to actually make the container, it's often easier than you might think. A great bark basket to try first is my favorite, commonly known as a "berry bucket." You can make this bucket style short and wide to act like a basket, or long and slender for a nice arrow quiver that's already camouflaged to match the local forest (nothing blends in with bark like more bark). The only limits are the flexibility of the peeled bark and your creativity.

STEP 1 Scratch or compress a football shape on the inside center area of your freshly peeled or thoroughly rehydrated tree bark.

STEP 2 Etch this shape in the middle of your bark, with the "points" of the football just touching each edge of the bark. Fold the bark in half, allowing the scored section to bend freely.

STEP 3 The shape you made will bend inward, and the cylindrical vessel will be complete when you tie the bucket together with cord or rope.

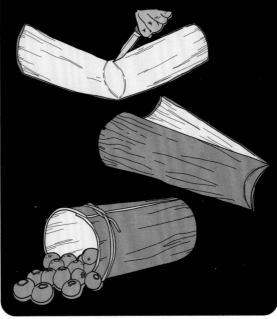

HEARTY VENISON SOUP

SERVES 6 TO 8

Most people assume that the word "venison" always refers to deer meat, yet in native language, it can be more closely translated to "meat from the hunt" (and this wouldn't always be deer meat). Today, the word venison is engrained in our language as the red meat from wild deer, and just a few New World species provide the bulk of the venison consumed in the United States. This nourishing meat has a history of feeding the people of this land, all the way back to the most remote times. In keeping with the traditions of many First Nation cultures, a pot full of venison soup is still a welcome sight when walking into camp (or coming home after a long hard day at work).

FOR THE VENISON:

- 1½ **pounds (0.5 kg) venison, cut into 1-inch (2.5 cm) cubes**
- 2 **teaspoons (10 g) seasoned salt**
- 2 **tablespoons (30 ml) canola oil**
- 2 **cups (480 ml) vegetable broth**

FOR THE SOUP:

- 8 **ounces (225 g) wild rice**
- 1 **tablespoon (15 ml) canola oil**
- 2 **medium carrots, diced**
- 2 **medium leeks, rinsed and sliced**
- 1 **cup (50 g) chopped wild onions**
- 7 **cups (1.7 l) vegetable broth**
- 1 **(15.8-ounce) (470-ml) can Great Northern beans, drained**
- 1 **(14.5-ounce) (428-ml) can fire-roasted tomatoes**
- 1 **teaspoon (0.5 g) dried thyme**
- 2 **bay leaves**
- ¼ **teaspoon (1 g) ground cinnamon**
- 1 **teaspoon (5 g) kosher salt**
- ½ **teaspoon (1 g) black pepper**
- **Sour cream and fresh chopped flat-leaf parsley, for serving**

1. Make the venison: In a bowl toss the venison with seasoned salt to coat. In a large saucepan heat oil over medium heat; add the venison and sear on all sides, about 5 minutes total. Add broth, scraping the bottom of pan. Reduce heat to low. Simmer, covered, until venison is tender, about 1 hour 30 minutes.

2. Make the soup: Meanwhile, in a medium stockpot cook rice over medium-high, stirring constantly, until rice begins to pop, 3 to 5 minutes. Stir in oil, carrots, leeks, and onions. Cook until vegetables are browned, about 5 minutes. Add broth, beans, tomatoes, thyme, bay leaves, cinnamon, salt, and pepper; stir to combine. Simmer, uncovered, until rice is tender, about 45 minutes. Remove and discard bay leaves.

3. When venison is tender, use a slotted spoon to transfer to the soup. Top servings with sour cream and parsley.

TOUGHER CUTS OF VENISON REQUIRE A LITTLE MORE COOKING TIME THAN OTHERS TO ENSURE THE FINISHED STEW WILL BE TENDER.

101 BROWSE NATURE'S GROCERY STORE

The wild holds a veritable cornucopia of edible fruits, berries, nuts, and more. Take a look at this chart to find out a little about each of the many offerings you can find in the wild that can provide a good amount of calories to your diet.

ACORNS

CALORIES 475 calories per cup (125 g)

NUTRIENTS Contains vitamin B6, folate, copper, and manganese

WHERE Woodland and temperate habitats throughout the northern hemisphere

WHEN Autumn, with nuts sometimes wintering over into spring

TIPS Remove the shells and soak in water to remove tannic acid

WILD STRAWBERRY

CALORIES 45 calories per cup (200 g)

NUTRIENTS One cup of berries will give you more than a full day's supply of vitamin C

WHERE Woodland areas in North America

WHEN A very short season in late spring

TIPS Don't be confused by the Indian strawberry, which is edible but completely flavorless

CRANBERRY

CALORIES 46 calories per cup (100 g)

NUTRIENTS One cup contains one-fifth of your daily requirement of vitamin C

WHERE Acidic bogs and wetland areas in northern latitudes

WHEN Berries ripen to red in autumn

TIPS Eating the berries is a widely used remedy to treat and prevent urinary tract infections

BLACKBERRY

CALORIES 62 calories per cup (100 g)

NUTRIENTS A cup has 50% of your daily vitamin C and 36% of your vitamin K

WHERE Open ground and woodland edges throughout the northern hemisphere

WHEN Early to the middle of summer

TIPS Blackberry leaves can be dried and steeped as a tea that has a mild taste and helps treat diarrhea

BLACK WALNUT

CALORIES 760 calories per cup (125 g)

NUTRIENTS Significant amounts of magnesium, phosphorus, and copper

WHERE Old fields and forests in the eastern half of North America

WHEN The nuts are fully formed in early autumn and may stay good well into winter

TIPS Outer husks can be used for dye and a tea that acts as a deworming medicine

ELDERBERRY

CALORIES 106 calories per cup (100 g)

NUTRIENTS The berries are high in vitamin B6, vitamin C, calcium, iron, and potassium

WHERE Sunny areas throughout the northern hemisphere

WHEN Early to midsummer

TIPS Don't munch on the leaves, stem, or green berries; most parts are toxic except for the ripe berries

DANDELION

CALORIES 25 calories per cup (75 g)

NUTRIENTS Loaded with vitamins A, C, and K, along with a small amount of most other necessary minerals

WHERE Disturbed ground, lawns, fields, and open areas worldwide

WHEN Year-round

TIPS Use yellow flower heads in a salad or roast the roots as a coffee alternative

RASPBERRY

CALORIES 64 calories per cup (125 g)

NUTRIENTS One cup has 54% of your daily vitamin C and 12% of your daily vitamin K

WHERE Open areas throughout the northern hemisphere

WHEN Early to the middle of summer

TIPS Raspberries are a close relative of the blackberry, and their leaves can also make a tea

CHERRY

CALORIES 77 calories per cup (150 g)

NUTRIENTS 40% of your daily requirement of vitamin A and 26% of your vitamin C; and some potassium, copper, and manganese

WHERE Forest edges and old fields throughout the northern hemisphere

WHEN Early, mid, or late summer, depending on the species

TIPS Don't swallow cherry pits or eat the leaves, as these are poisonous

ROSE HIPS

CALORIES 162 calories per cup (100 g)

NUTRIENTS One cup provides the vitamins A, C, E, and K, as well as some calcium, magnesium, and manganese

WHERE Sunny areas throughout the northern hemisphere

WHEN Early fall

TIPS Rose hips are a powerhouse when it comes to vitamin C, containing seven times your daily allowance in one cup

PERSIMMON

CALORIES 127 calories per cup (225 g)

NUTRIENTS One cup provides a full day's vitamin C

WHERE Old fields and transition areas throughout the eastern and central U.S.

WHEN Early to mid-fall

TIPS Pick only the wrinkled and gooey fruits; unripe ones give you a strong case of cotton mouth

WILD RICE

CALORIES 170 calories per cup (250 g)

NUTRIENTS Traces of many vitamins and minerals, and 7 grams of protein

WHERE Wetlands throughout the northern U.S. and southern Canada

WHEN Early fall

TIPS Harvest from an open canoe, bending the seed heads into the boat and tapping them with a stick

PAW PAW

CALORIES 80 calories per cup (150 g)

NUTRIENTS One cup has 18% of your daily recommended vitamin C and about 10% of your daily potassium

WHERE Floodplains and forests throughout the eastern and central U.S.

WHEN Late summer or very early fall

TIPS The wood is excellent for frictions, fire material, and the bark can be used as tinder and cordage

AMARANTH

CALORIES 716 calories per cup (250 g)

NUTRIENTS There are 26 grams of protein, 30% of your daily calcium, and a full day's iron in one cup

WHERE Fields and open ground throughout North America

WHEN Late summer or early fall

TIPS Seeds can be boiled into a cooked grain or ground into flour; the leaves are edible raw or cooked

BLUEBERRY

CALORIES 84 calories per cup (100 g)

NUTRIENTS One cup contains one-quarter of your daily vitamin C and one-third of your vitamin K

WHERE These bushes and their relatives can grow in a wide range of temperate climates

WHEN Mid to late summer

TIPS Regular consumption is believed to improve vision, and eating dried berries can help stop diarrhea

GRAPES

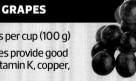

CALORIES 100 calories per cup (100 g)

NUTRIENTS Wild grapes provide good amounts of vitamin C, vitamin K, copper, and potassium

WHERE Woods and wood edges throughout the northern hemisphere

WHEN Midsummer to mid-fall

TIPS Grapes have one to four teardrop-shape seeds; the toxic moonseed has only one seed, which is curved and flat

ELK CHILI

SERVES 6 TO 8

At the heart of any chili dish, we inevitably find chili powder. This reddish dust is based on the dried and ground fruit of one (or multiple) varieties of chile pepper. As a common adjunct, you'll also encounter cumin and paprika, along with a few other spices, depending on the recipe. There are plenty of variations of this spice blend, and no shortage of myths surrounding the origin of chili. In one fiery story, a lovely Spanish nun named Sister Mary of Agreda went into a trance-like state and emerged with the recipe we know as chili con carne. Other accounts brand chili as the "soup of the devil" for its ability to inflame the passions. In any case, chili showcases many different ingredients and regional styles.

6	strips thick-cut bacon, chopped
2½	pounds (1 kg) elk steak, cut into ¾-inch cubes
1	tablespoon (15 g) all-purpose flour
6	cups (1.5 l) water
2	small yellow onions, chopped
2½	cups (600 ml) tomato sauce
¼	cup (135 g) chili powder
¼	cup (60 ml) white vinegar
1	tablespoon (15 ml) light molasses
1	tablespoon (15 g) unsweetened cocoa powder
2	teaspoons (5 g) cumin
2	teaspoons (4.5 g) paprika
2	teaspoons (2 g) dried oregano
1	teaspoon (3 g) garlic powder
1	teaspoon (2 g) ground allspice
1	teaspoon (2 g) black pepper
1	teaspoon (5 g) salt
1	(15-ounce) (443-ml) can dark kidney beans, rinsed and drained
1	(15-ounce) can black beans, rinsed and drained
	Shredded cheese and sliced green onions
	Crackers and hot sauce, for serving

1. In a large Dutch oven cook bacon over medium-high heat until crisp. Use a slotted spoon to transfer bacon to a paper-towel-lined plate to drain.

2. Add elk to the Dutch oven. Cook, stirring often, until browned, 8 to 10 minutes. Stir in flour. Cook, stirring constantly, 5 minutes more. Add the water, onions, tomato sauce, chili powder, vinegar, molasses, cocoa powder, cumin, paprika, oregano, garlic powder, allspice, black pepper, and salt. Stir to combine.

3. Bring chili to boiling; reduce heat. Simmer, uncovered, for 3 hours, stirring occasionally. Stir in beans the last 45 minutes of cooking.

4. Top with shredded cheese and green onions. Serve chili with crackers and hot sauce.

YOU CAN USE SHREDDED CHEDDAR TO COVER A HEAPING BOWL OF THIS CHUNKY CHILI—OR TRY A SPICY CHEESE. PEPPER JACK IS ONE OF MY FAVORITE CHEESES FOR THIS PURPOSE.

102 MAKE SOME BACON

Anyone can make homemade bacon! Just gather these simple ingredients. Get 3 pounds (1.25 kg) of thick, skinless pork belly; ½ cup (100 g) white sugar; 1 tablespoon (15 ml) maple syrup; 2 tablespoons (30 g) coarse salt; 1 teaspoon (5 g) curing salt; a 2-gallon (7.5-l) freezer storage bag; and some coarse crushed black pepper (to coat the bacon). Mix the wet and dry ingredients (except for the pepper) until well blended. Place the meat and the mix into the freezer bag, and massage the contents around until you have coated the pork evenly. Place the bag in the fridge, and massage the pork once daily for the next seven days. After a week, check the meat for soft spots. When fully cured, it will be firm to the touch everywhere. Add another sprinkle of salt and wait a few more days, if soft. Once cured, rinse and dry the meat, coat it in crushed pepper, and smoke it for the signature smoked flavor. Make sure it reaches 150°F (65°C) for safety. Slice it into strips, and your bacon is complete.

103 PARCH YOUR CORN

This unusual Native American food was once a common snack among First Nation peoples, and later copied by settlers, mountain men, and trappers. This rudimentary form of popcorn is easy to make, tasty, filling, and lightweight—perfect for trail food. You can also grind parched corn into a rough cornmeal and then boil it to make a traditional corn soup. To make your own, you'll need a skillet, fine salt, some animal fat (pig fat is a colonial tradition), and some dried sweet corn. This last item is the only tricky ingredient to get, but it's the best type of corn for this food. Melt a little fat in your skillet over medium heat (over the campfire or your home cooktop), dump in enough dried corn to barely cover the bottom of the skillet, and start stirring. Keep it up, stirring the greasy corn until it starts to swell up and make little popping noises. Stir until all of the corn kernels are golden brown. Add salt to the corn and you're done! Parched corn can last for months in a cloth or paper bag.

TIM'S TOP 10

104 FEAST ON WILD FOODS

When it comes to hunting and gathering wild food, there are a lot of herbs, vegetables, roots, berries, fish, game, and even bugs and mollusks that we can enjoy. These traditional wild foods can be nutritional, delicious, easy to find, easy to prepare, or simply an abundant resource. These are 10 of my favorite wild foods, and I encourage you to try them all!

1 RABBIT So tender and so chicken-flavored, rabbit meat is easy to adapt into familiar meals and dishes. Rabbits may be hunted or trapped, and they can be plentiful in the right habitats.

2 TROUT There are many species of this cold-water fish genus, and most are mild and delicate. Trout can be elusive to catch with plenty of tiny bones, but these fish are still excellent food.

3 SASSAFRAS The unique pattern of leaves (three different primary leaf shapes) seems to match the unique flavor of the roots on this native tree. Sassafras roots make an outstanding tea.

4 MAPLE SYRUP A traditional Native American sweetener, maple syrup is rich and sweet. Various species of maple can be used, and this sweetener is especially good in sassafras tea. Just 2-tablespoons (30 ml) of real syrup has 100 calories with high riboflavin and manganese.

5 HICKORY NUTS The non-bitter nuts from trees in the genus *Carya* are the most calorie-dense wild plant food. Just 1 ounce (28 g) of shelled hickory nut packs more than 190 calories and a sweet taste.

6 BLACKBERRIES Easy to identify and found all around the northern hemisphere, blackberries and their relatives are delicious and loaded with vitamins and minerals.

7 WATERCRESS This spicy wild plant has tender leaves that are packed with sharp, peppery flavors. It is often found growing in clear springs and streams, and can be eaten in many different ways.

8 ACORNS These nuts are the seeds of oak trees, and while they aren't exactly delicious (they are bitter before processing and bland afterward), they can be a plentiful and sustaining staple food (providing up to 2,000 calories per pound (450 g)).

9 DEER Several deer species can be found throughout North America, and many others are found across the globe. The dark red meat known as venison is both tasty and nutritious.

10 SQUIRREL I've called it the "chicken of the trees" for good reason. The mild white meat is similar to rabbit, and very close in flavor to chicken. These muscular little mammals are delicious!

MIDWESTERN MOOSE MEAT LOAF

SERVES 8

It's been said that you need three things to eat a moose. The first is a big gun, to harvest the massive moose. The second is a big knife, to process the creature. The third, and just as important as the other two, is a big recipe book to give you dozens of different ways to eat several hundred pounds of monotonous moose meat. Moose is very similar to beef, though it's a little gamier, tougher, and much leaner that your typical beef cattle (especially the cows from a feed lot). You won't find fat marbling in moose meat, but you'll have plenty of meat to work with. Large males can easily exceed half a ton (1,000 pounds) and yield hundreds of pounds of useable meat, all of which can be turned into moose meat loaf!

FOR THE MEAT LOAF:

1	medium yellow onion, finely chopped
1	large green bell pepper, finely chopped
1	cup (90 g) quick-cooking rolled oats
¾	cup (180 ml) applesauce
1	large egg, lightly beaten
1	teaspoon (5 g) salt
1	teaspoon (3 g) garlic powder
½	teaspoon (1 g) white pepper
½	teaspoon (3 g) celery salt
2	pounds (900 g) ground moose
3	ounces (85 g) Wisconsin cheddar cheese cut into ½-inch (12-mm) cubes

FOR THE GLAZE:

½	cup (120 ml) ketchup
1	tablespoon (15 ml) yellow mustard
2	teaspoons (10 ml) Worcestershire sauce

1. Make the meat loaf: Preheat oven to 350°F (175°C). Line a rimmed baking sheet with parchment paper. In a large bowl combine the onion, green pepper, oats, applesauce, egg, salt, garlic powder, white pepper, and celery salt. Add ground moose; using clean hands, mix until combined (do not overmix). Lightly pat the mixture into 9x5-inch (23x13-cm) loaf and place on prepared baking sheet.

2. Using clean fingers, gently press cheese cubes into meat loaf, at least ½ inch (12 mm) deep. Gently reform loaf to fill holes.

3. Make the glaze: In a small bowl stir together ketchup, mustard, and Worcestershire sauce. Spoon half of the glaze over the loaf.

4. Bake the meat loaf for 45 minutes. Spread remaining glaze over loaf. Bake until a thermometer reads 160°F (70°C), 15 to 20 minutes more. Let stand 10 minutes before serving.

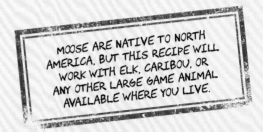

MOOSE ARE NATIVE TO NORTH AMERICA, BUT THIS RECIPE WILL WORK WITH ELK, CARIBOU, OR ANY OTHER LARGE GAME ANIMAL AVAILABLE WHERE YOU LIVE.

105 IMPROVISE A FISH WEIR

Fish traps have been used by people around the world for a very long time; the biggest such trap is the fish weir. Since these traps are working hard to collect food for you day and night, they can really make an impact on your food gathering efforts.

So if you want to get serious about fishing, and you're going to be in one spot for a while, add a fish weir to your food collection plan. A weir can be a V-shape wall or a circular fence that either directs fish into smaller fish traps or simply confines them within the weir. Some of the traditional weir construction styles of ancient times are still used today.

Weirs can be built of stone for permanent construction. They can also be made by driving stakes into the mud to create semipermanent installations. Your weir can take advantage of the flow of a river. And in coastal areas, they can work with the tides– trapping fish as the tide goes out. Weirs can get you as close as you're going to get to "shooting fish in a barrel" in a primitive survival setting.

106 USE YOUR BARE HANDS

The concept of "hand fishing" is simple enough, but it's like many other "simple" survival skills in that it actually requires a lot of technique. Whether graveling for catfish or bug diving to collect lobsters, you're taking a page from the playbook of our most remote ancestors when you catch aquatic animals with your bare hands.

CATCH A CAT Catfish like to hang out in underwater rock ledges, as well as in holes and under submerged logs. If you reach into these protected spots, the fish will be trapped with its back up against the wall. If all goes right, the fish will advance and bite your hand. Fight your natural urge to pull your hand away; leave your hand in the fish's mouth and pull it toward you. Wrap your free arm around the fish, being careful to avoid contact with the barbs on the fish's fins.

BAG A BUG Likewise, speedy grabs and swatting motions are the most successful methods of snatching a lobster from protected spots in shallow saltwater. Of course, these underwater shelters can also contain sea urchins, moray eels, scorpion fish, and other sea creatures that bite, stab, and sting. Being truly bare-handed is a poor choice. Instead, don a pair of Kevlar gloves. These cut-proof, puncture-proof gauntlets protect against urchin spines and many other dangers of the deep. And never go hand-fishing alone. You'll want some help if you get injured or your arm is trapped underwater.

107 DIG UP DINNER

All around the world, tasty treats can be found for the price of a little digging. Clams, mussels, and similarly shelled creatures are often buried in sand or mud, and all you need to harvest them is a pail, a shovel, and a bit of knowledge.

Start by doing your homework on these creatures—find out what's locally abundant, what's in season, and what may be toxic to eat or illegal to collect in your area. Then put on your waders and go digging. The hints that follow are for clams, but many of their relatives can be harvested the same way.

Clams are chewy, rich buried treasures that can be found in tidal saltwater areas across the globe. Other related species make their home in fresh or brackish water. Many are prized for their size and flavor.

For example, the U.S. west coast is home to razor and geoduck clams along with many species of bay clams and other mollusks. Eastern clams include the Atlantic surf and soft-shell, among others. Regardless of the location, most of these creatures can be unearthed from their sandy nests using the same guidelines.

GUIDELINES

FIND THE RIGHT SPOT Learn where your local clam beds are located, and try to discover the "hot spots" in those areas.

GO AT LOW TIDE This means more area to successfully dig. Minus tides are best—get there two hours before peak low tide. During times of less swell, your quarry is likely to be closer to the surface. And closer to the surface means closer to your plate.

LOOK FOR SIGNS A clam's neck near the surface of the sand will produce a distinct "show." Look for small holes, round dimples, or indentations in dry sand, or pound your shovel handle in receding surf. If you're lucky, the pounding will reveal a show—or two.

DIG FAST Some clams are sluggish creatures, but others are lightning fast. The Pacific razor clam is one of the fastest diggers, and it can bury itself faster than some clammers can dig.

108 GET A LINE ON CRABS

The ideal way to catch crabs is with a crab pot (which works on the same principle as a standard fish trap), but making one isn't easy. Luckily, crabs can also be caught with a simple handheld baited line.

Just tie a piece of bait, such as a chicken leg, to the end of a weighted line. The weight needs to be heavy enough to drag the bait to the bottom even in a current. Cast the baited line roughly 4–6 feet (1–2 m) out into the water. This short line helps with easy retrieval and avoids wasting time while you battle the currents. Now wait—and remember, patience is a virtue.

When a crab grips the bait, you'll notice the line tightening. Don't yank the line or lift the crab from the water! Haul it in very slowly until the crab is visible—only a rare one will hang on aggressively enough to make it to dry land, so be sure you have a dip net handy. Try this technique off jetties and piers for the best chances.

CRAWFISH BOIL WITH CREOLE SACHET

SERVES 4

I didn't know it at the time, but the first crawfish boil I ever attended was done right. I was a young teaching assistant for Frank and Karen Sherwood, owners of the primitive living school Earthwalk Northwest. I helped them with their classes, and in turn they would teach me some new skills and feed me (very well, I might add). After one particularly long day, we covered a large table with many layers of newspaper. Nothing had prepared me for the sight and smell of Frank dumping out a huge pot of spiced crawfish, sausage, potatoes, and corn on the cob onto the table. There were no plates and little elbow room as the students and staff joined together for a very memorable feast. Thank you, Sherwoods. This recipe is dedicated to you!

6	pounds (2.7 kg) fresh crawfish
1	tablespoon (15 g) mustard seeds
2	teaspoons (3.5 g) coriander seeds
2	teaspoons (2 g) whole allspice
2	teaspoons (4.5 g) dill seed
1	teaspoon (0.5 g) dried thyme
1	teaspoon (2 g) whole cloves
1	teaspoon (1 g) crushed red pepper
¾	cup (215 g) kosher salt
2	oranges, halved
3	lemons, halved
6	bay leaves
1	head garlic, unpeeled, cloves separated
6	new potatoes
4	ears corn, husked and halved
1	large yellow onion, cut into 6 wedges
1	pound (450 g) andouille sausage, cut into 1-inch (2.5-cm) pieces
	Hot sauce

1. Rinse the crawfish thoroughly in the bag in which they arrived to remove dirt and mud. Put the crawfish in a large container and fill with cool water. Stir to remove dirt from the crawfish. Transfer small batches of crawfish to a colander and rinse under cool running water. Pick out any debris or dead crawfish. Once all crawfish have been rinsed, discard dirty water, and return the crawfish to the container. Repeat this process 6 to 8 times, or until the water is clear.

2. For the spice bags, combine mustard, coriander, allspice, dill, thyme, cloves, and crushed red pepper in a cloth tea bag; securely tie closed.

3. Fill a 20-quart (19-l) pot with 3 gallons (11.5 l) of water. Add the salt, spice bag, oranges, lemons, bay leaves, and garlic. Cover and bring to boiling over high heat. Reduce heat and simmer, covered, for 15 minutes.

4. Add potatoes, corn, onion, and sausage to the pot. Cook, covered, 10 minutes. Add crawfish and return to a boil. Cook, covered, for 3 minutes. Turn off the heat and let stand, covered, for 10 minutes. (Crawfish will turn bright red and the body and tail pull apart easily.) Drain well and serve with hot sauce.

109 WORK FOR SCALE

Whether by trap, by hook, or by hand, you have caught one or more fish to satisfy your hunger. Now you need to clean the animals and prepare them for cooking. Fish are the easiest animal to skin and gut, but there are a few ways to make things go more smoothly.

Most fish have some sort of scales; they're there to protect the fish against all kinds of injuries. Their toughness also makes them difficult to digest, should you decide to eat the fish as-is. You can always fillet your fish and remove the skin completely, but removing only the scales will preserve the valuable calories stored in the skin. Keeping the skin also helps to preserve the

fat contained in the fish, which is important for both flavor and nutrition.

You can purchase simple fish-scaling tools, or you can improvise them on the spot: Use a knife, a sharp stone flake, or shells. You can also screw bottle caps to a stick or strip of wood to create a toothed scaler. Whatever you use, just scrape the fish from tail to head to begin removing scales, preferably before gutting. When you don't feel or see any more scales coming off, scrape your fingernails from tail to head to check for stragglers, and scrape again as needed.

110 FINISH THE JOB

Now for the part you've been waiting for: gutting the fish. It's a very easy task, especially with a sharp blade.

You can remove the head by chopping it off, and you're free to snip off the fins, but these steps are certainly not necessary. Don't waste the organs you remove, as they make great fish bait and trap bait. Don't discard the head, either—use it for soup stock to make a broth full of minerals and good fish flavor.

STEP 1 Cut into the fish's underside, starting between the gills and slicing down to the anal vent. It's okay if your knife tip slices through a few organs—fish aren't that germy.

STEP 2 Now use one or two fingers to swipe out the innards, and you're basically done for head-still-on cleaning. You can use your thumbnail to scrape the body cavity of blood and leftover entrails.

STEP 3 It's also a good idea to rinse the fish out. Rinse it quickly in cold water, and then keep it out of water for firmer flesh. Store on ice or cook immediately.

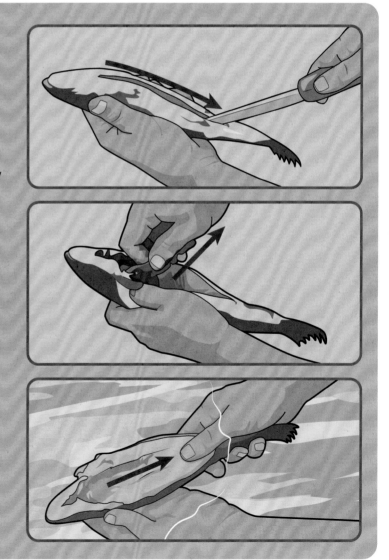

111 LEARN HOW TO FILLET

Bigger fish will yield some big, beautiful fillets, and cutting your own is a great way to portion out a larger catch. This process will differ depending on the fish and its particular bone structure, but here's one way to get started.

STEP 1 Use a sharp, flexible fillet knife to make a deep cut behind the gill plate and at the tail on one side of your fish.

STEP 2 Make a connecting cut down the fish's back to join the gill cut and tail cut.

STEP 3 Begin slicing down the fish, using the backbones as a guide. Make long cuts from head to tail, eventually cutting down to the belly, and peel off the fillet. If you have not gutted the fish, be careful to avoid piercing the body cavity.

STEP 4 Repeat the process on the other side of the fish.

STEP 5 Waste not, want not. Remove the innards, chop up the remaining fish, and simmer in water to create a savory fish stew.

112 SKIP THE PREP WORK

Fish with tiny scales and sparsely scaled fish can be gutted and prepared immediately–no scaling necessary. I am a big fan of trout with the scales still on, as well as catfish and smaller fish that I'm lucky enough to catch in small traps. These finger-size fish don't even need to be gutted. Fry them or roast them whole, ideally until they are crispy, and crunch on them (bones and all) like a kind of fishy cracker.

COUNTRY-FRIED CATFISH WITH POLENTA

SERVES 4

These spiny whiskered fish aren't just caught in the wild. They're readily adaptable to fish farming. Our family farm primarily yielded cattle and crops, but when I was a teen, we tried our own catfish farm one summer. My father cut a large steel tank in half (lengthwise) and pulled it into a shady location. The tank was soon filled with water and little catfish (available from a pond stocking company). We fed the catfish with commercial fish pellets, table scraps, and even dog food (when the farmer's co-op was out of fish food). Over the span of a few months, the fish were big enough to eat and they were delicious! This recipe is a nod to my dad's agricultural creativity and my mom's ability to coat anything in cornmeal (and then fry it to perfection).

FOR THE FISH:

4   skinless catfish fillets (about 6 ounces (175 g) each)
1½ cups (360 ml) buttermilk
1   teaspoon (5 g) salt, divided
    Vegetable oil for frying
1   cup (140 g) cornmeal
1   cup (120 g) all-purpose flour
2   teaspoons (10 g) Cajun seasoning
½   teaspoon (2 g) ground oregano
    Chopped fresh parsley, pickled jalapeños, and lemon wedges

FOR THE POLENTA:

3   cups (720 ml) water
1   cup (240 ml) heavy cream
1   cup (140 g) polenta (corn grits)
½   cup (45 g) grated Parmesan cheese
3   tablespoons (50 g) unsalted butter
2   jalapeños, seeded and diced
1   teaspoon (5 g) salt
½   teaspoon (1 g) black pepper

1. Make the fish: Thaw fish, if frozen. Rinse fish; pat dry with paper towels. In a large shallow dish stir together the buttermilk and ½ teaspoon (2.5 g) salt. Add the fillets and turn to coat. Cover and refrigerate for 1 to 2 hours. Prepare the polenta while the fish is soaking.

2. Make the polenta: In a medium saucepan bring water and cream to boiling over medium-high heat. Slowly pour polenta into the water mixture, whisking constantly to prevent lumps. Reduce heat to low, whisking often, until polenta starts to thicken, about 5 minutes. Cook, covered, stirring occasionally, until creamy and spoonable, 30 minutes. Remove from heat. Stir in Parmesan cheese, butter, jalapeños, salt, and black pepper until cheese is melted.

3. When ready, in a large cast-iron or heavy skillet heat 1 inch (2.5 cm) oil over high heat until a deep-fry thermometer reads 350°F (175°C). (Adjust the heat to maintain the temperature.)

4. In another shallow dish whisk together the cornmeal, flour, Cajun seasoning, remaining ½ teaspoon (2.5 g) salt, and oregano. Remove fish from the buttermilk, allowing excess buttermilk to drip from fillets. Coat both sides of the fillets in the cornmeal mixture. Set coated fillets on a wire rack to rest 5 to 10 minutes. In batches, carefully add the fillets to the hot oil. Fry until golden brown, 3 to 4 minutes per side. Transfer to a wire rack while frying remaining fillets.

5. Serve catfish alongside polenta. Sprinkle with parsley and serve with pickled jalapeños and lemon wedges.

113 BUILD A SMOKER

Virtually any box, container, or tiny shed can become a smoker for fish, meats, and even animal hides. Take what you have available, and turn it into a serious smoke box.

APPLIANCE-BOX SMOKER

Use a giant cardboard box or crate from a new appliance to create a cold smoker. Cut out the bottom or leave it open on bare ground. Use sticks or metal rods poked through the box to make a rack for the food. You can even use wire to dangle your catch from the ceiling of the box. Cut a door in the side, and place a pan of coals and wood chips on the ground inside. You can also use a hot plate and a pan of damp wood chips.

ELECTRIC-RANGE SMOKER

Repurpose an old electric range into a smoker by cutting a hole in the bottom of the oven compartment and using the metal drawer to hold your pan of coals and wood chips. For an easier approach, just place a pan of coals in the bottom of the oven compartment and use the existing oven racks to hold your fish or food.

PERMANENT SMOKE HOUSE

Build or repurpose a very small shed for hot or cold smoking. Stove piping or a clay drain line can be used to pipe smoke into the structure, and the smoke can be supplied by an old woodstove or a similar fire box.

114 SMOKE YOUR CATCH

While it is possible to smoke smaller fish whole, filleting and hanging them properly allows them to smoke more evenly, as the greater exposed surface area lets the smoke penetrate deeper into the flesh. And when you're dealing with larger fish, this step becomes a necessity.

Cut small fish along the backbone and press them flat. These flattened fillets can be hung on rods, laid out flat on a rack, or draped over a pole.

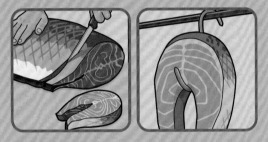

Cut larger fish, like salmon, into U-shape steaks and hang them on hooks in your smoker.

115 PRESERVE FISH WITH SMOKE

Now that you've caught some fish, it's time to figure out what to do with them. Before the days of freezers and canners, smoking, drying, and brining techniques were used to preserve the catch. Today, we can use some of these long-perfected practices to preserve and season the catch of the day.

Smoking fish can produce some remarkably flavorful results, and it can be done without much in the way of modern conveniences. There are two traditional ways (using the same setup) to smoke fish and other foods.

HOT SMOKING This technique uses a closed box to hold in the smoke and the heat. The fish is cooked by this heat and permeated with a smoky flavor. Fish prepared in this manner can last up to a week at room temperature.

COLD SMOKING Cold smoking is done at cooler temperatures for a longer period of time. The goal in this method is long-term fish storage, which requires the fish be dried rather than cooked. It should not get hot enough in the smoker to actually cook the fish: temperatures under 100°F (38°C) are ideal.

HOT-SMOKED TROUT WITH MUSTARD, DILL, AND CAPER SAUCE

SERVES 4

The smoking of fish is an ancient form of food preservation that can be done in two ways: cold smoking and hot smoking. For long-term storage, cold smoking will give the food maximum longevity. Hot smoking is more commonly done for short-term storage and as a delicious cooking method. When combined with brining and some savory seasonings, as we'll share in this recipe, you'll forget that the trout spent its life in frigid and flavorless waters.

FOR THE FISH:
- ½   **cup (140 g) kosher salt**
- ½   **cup (100 g) brown sugar**
- 4   **whole trout, gutted and gilled**
    Lemon wedges

FOR THE SAUCE:
- ¾   **cup (180 ml) spicy brown mustard**
- ½   **cup (100 g) sugar**
- ⅓   **cup (80 ml) fresh lemon juice**
- 1   **tablespoon (6.5 g) dry mustard**
- ¾   **cup (180 ml) vegetable oil**
- ¾   **cup (90 g) drained capers**
- ½   **cup (9 g) chopped fresh dill**
- ½   **teaspoon (1 g) black pepper**

1. Make the fish: In a gallon of water stir together the salt and sugar until dissolved. Submerge the trout. Refrigerate, covered, for at least 2 hours and up to overnight.

2. Remove the trout from the brine and pat dry with paper towels. Place trout on a rack set over a baking sheet; refrigerate for at least a few hours and up to overnight.

3. Turn the smoker on to maintain a temperature between 215°F and 225°F (102°C and 107°C). Place trout on the smoking racks, skin-side down and at least ¼ inch (6 mm) apart. Cook for 2 hours or until a thermometer inserted in fish reads 145°F. (Do not let the temperature get above 225°F.)

4. Make the sauce: In a medium bowl stir together the spicy mustard, sugar, lemon juice, and dry mustard. Gradually whisk in the oil. Stir in capers, dill, and black pepper.

5. Serve the trout with the sauce and lemon wedges.

TROUT IS WIDELY REGARDED AS ONE OF THE BEST FISH FOR SMOKING, BUT OTHER SMALL FISH CAN BE COOKED USING THIS SAME TECHNIQUE.

116 MAKE JERKY

Before refrigeration and canning, humans figured out how to dry meats as jerky. Most of us think about beef jerky, but any lean meat can and should be used. Turkey, for instance, is naturally lean and mildly flavored, making it perfect for seasoned jerky. Nearly any hunted game and fish can be turned into jerky following a few easy steps.

STEP 1 Select a lean cut of meat. The less fat, the better, so go for a lean sirloin or similar cut.

STEP 2 Remove all visible fat (fat makes the jerky spoil faster), then cut the meat into thin strips no thicker than ½ inch (13 mm). If you're buying meat from a market, ask the butcher to cut the strips for you. Otherwise, freeze the meat for 5 minutes to make it easier to cut on your own.

STEP 3 Marinate the strips of meat with olive oil and sea salt or a recipe of your choice, then let them refrigerate overnight.

STEP 4 Rub dry spices over the marinated cuts before baking. Don't be afraid to experiment, and don't shy away from salt—it will aid in the drying process.

STEP 5 If you're lucky, you have a dehydrator for this step. But if you don't, your oven will suffice: Preheat it to 165°F (74°C). Remember, the goal is to dry, not cook. Set the strips atop a wire rack in the oven, and catch any drippings. Then bake 1 to 3 hours, or until the jerky is dry to the touch.

STEP 6 You should eat your jerky within two weeks of making it. Store it in an airtight container (a vacuum sealer is ideal) and refrigerate until ready to eat.

117 PUT THE CHIPS DOWN

You won't be smoking anything without a good source of smoke, which means that wood chips are the most vital part of the operation. A modern smoking setup can involve a hot plate (portable electric burner) heating a pan of dampened chips. More traditional methods (sans electricity) involve a pan of hardwood coals from a fire with wet wood chips sprinkled over the top. Determine your method based on your nearby tree species.

Make sure you avoid any local species that are toxic. My local bad guys in the eastern U.S. are black locust, yew, buckeye, horse chestnut, rhododendron, and mountain laurel. You'll also want to skip bitter resinous woods like cedar, cypress, redwood, fir, pine, spruce, and other needle-bearing trees.

TREE	FLAVOR
APPLE	Apple wood, found in orchards, makes a sweet smoke perfect for poultry and pork.
HICKORY	Hickory chips produce a rich, sharp flavor and make hot, long-burning coals.
MAPLE	Chips from maple wood are excellent for smoking tasty cheeses.
MESQUITE	Native to the southern U.S., mesquite wood produces smoke with an earthy flavor.
ASH	Ash wood chips produce a lightly flavored smoke that's great for fish and poultry.
OAK	With a heavy smoke flavor, red oak is good on ribs and pork, and white oak yields lasting coals.

118 DRESS SMALL GAME

Even if you take your deer to the game processor for professional cutting and packaging, there's no reason you can't do the work yourself on rabbits, squirrels, and other small animals. Once you get the hang of it, you should be able to dress out a small animal in less than 10 minutes.

STEP 1 Take your legally hunted, trapped, or road-killed animal and your sharp knife to a clean wooden surface, like a board or a weathered, barkless log. Cut off the head and all four feet. The easiest way to do this is to use a small club of wood as a baton to strike the back of the knife blade and drive it through skin, muscle, tendon, and bone.

STEP 2 Lay the game on its back and set the knife edge above the anus. Tap the knife with the club to cut off the anus and tail. You could also cut a circle around the anus to isolate it, but this can be time-consuming and tricky on small game.

STEP 3 Make an incision in the belly skin and muscle starting at the sternum (breastbone) and cutting down to the anal cut. Slice shallowly, being careful to keep stomach and intestines whole. Scoop out the guts from liver to colon.

STEP 4 Now that the abdominal guts are gone, you can insert the knife into the chest cavity, blade edge up, and slice through the center of the rib cage all the way to the throat cut. Remove the heart and lungs (the only contents of the chest cavity). Save the "good" guts for sausage or soup. The lungs, heart, liver, and kidneys are definite keepers. If you're starving, flush out the stomach and intestines and cook those, too.

STEP 5 Peel off the hide. Start at the hind section, which is thinner and easier to remove. Work your thumb under the skin and cut it loose a little with the knife, if needed. Once you get a handful of hide, you can peel it off from tail to head (or where the head was formerly located). Save the skin for tanning, or scald the fur off with hot water and some scraping and use the skin for food.

STEP 6 Pick off any remaining hairs and give the carcass a rinse with clean water to remove blood and any dirt. Cook right away as a whole animal, or cut it into quarters with a little more baton work, then bread the quarters and fry them. You can also freeze the carcass in a vacuum-sealed plastic bag for later.

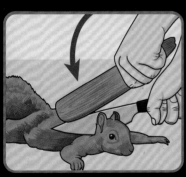

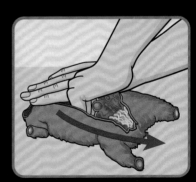

WILD GAME BREAKFAST SAUSAGE PATTIES

SERVES 8

The aroma of bacon may make us think of breakfast, but for me, a well-seasoned breakfast sausage is just as welcomed. When working with meats that gentle palates might consider "gamey," the classic sausage flavors of sage and black pepper are perennial favorites. These give us familiar flavors, and good ones at that. This recipe, however, has a few extras that also work well when blended into wild game meat. Dust off your meat grinder and purchase some fresh spices—we're about to give your breakfast bacon some competition.

2	pounds (900 g) wild game scrap meat (venison, moose, elk, or boar), well chilled
1/2	pound (450 g) pork fat back
1	tablespoon (15 g) kosher salt
1	tablespoon (15 g) dark brown sugar
2	teaspoons (10 g) ground sage
2	teaspoons (5 g) ground marjoram or oregano
1 1/2	teaspoons (6 g) coarse black pepper
1/2	teaspoon (1 g) paprika
1/4	teaspoon (0.5 g) ground cinnamon
2	tablespoons (30 ml) maple syrup

1. On a large die, run chilled meat and pork fat through a meat grinder.

2. Working quickly so the meat remains chilled, in a large bowl gently toss together ground meat with salt, brown sugar, sage, marjoram, black pepper, paprika, and cinnamon. Use your hands to incorporate spices thoroughly throughout the ground meat.

3. On a small die, regrind the seasoned meat. Drizzle meat with the maple syrup, and use your hands to incorporate throughout the ground meat. Shape meat into eight patties.

4. Heat an extra-large skillet over medium heat. Place the patties in the hot skillet, and cook until browned and a thermometer inserted in center reads 165°F (75°C), about 8 minutes, turning once halfway through cooking.

SAUSAGE-MAKING DATES BACK THOUSANDS OF YEARS AND WAS ORIGINALLY DEVISED AS A WAY TO PRESERVE MEAT (PARTICULARLY WHEN STUFFED INTO A CASING). YOU CAN USE SMALL-DIAMETER CASINGS TO CONVERT THE MEAT MIXTURE INTO SAVORY BREAKFAST LINKS.

WILD HERBS

1 ITCH AND STING CONTROL If you find yourself caught without a first-aid kit, there are many plants that can provide medicinal compounds and actions. The crushed leaves and stems of chickweed (*Stellaria media*) and crushed leaves of plantain (*Plantago major)* and others are great alternatives to calamine lotion for healing irritated skin and relieving itchiness. Plantain leaves crushed into a paste also works well on bee stings and other venomous bites, and this is the little plant called plantain that is in just about every yard in America. Just for clarification, this plant is not the banana-looking fruit called a plantain at stores.

2 WOUND TREATMENT Allantoin is a very special healing compound. It is found in the comfrey plant (*Symphytum officinale*) and several other plants (like plantain), and in the urine of cows and most other mammals. This useful substance is known for increasing the water content of the extracellular matrix of skin, and enhancing the flaking and peeling of upper layers of dead skin cells. This increases the smoothness of the skin, and promotes cell proliferation and wound healing. The funny thing is, you've probably already used allantoin. It is frequently added to toothpaste, mouthwash, and other modern-oral hygiene products.

3 INSECT REPELLENT Naturally occurring bug-repellent compounds may be foul or fragrant to our noses, but plants from both extremes can help us repel pests in the great outdoors. Pineapple weed (*Matricaria matricarioides*) is a small non-native plant found throughout the northern hemisphere, and the small, feathery leaves smell just like pineapple when crushed. These crushed leaves can also help to repel mosquitoes and other flying pests. Reapply every few hours for best results, since these plant aromas tend to dissipate quickly. And make sure you positively identify a plant before you touch it or crush it onto your skin.

6 COVERING HUMAN SCENT There are a surprising number of wild plants that can provide us with a powerful scent, one strong enough to cover our human scent during hunting and trapping activities. Wild onion (numerous species in the *Allium* genus) and related garlic-scented plants can be crushed on the skin and on trap parts as an effective cover scent to hide the strong smell of people. This olfactory camouflage can be accomplished with plenty of other nontoxic and strong-smelling plants. Pine needles, wild mint, and many other plants can confuse your quarry. But don't rub unknown plants on yourself if you have any doubt of the identity.

5 UPSET STOMACH Have you ever wondered why some restaurants treat you to a mint after your meal? There's some wisdom in this practice, and it's not for fresh breath. It's to settle your stomach after eating what was probably an overly large and greasy meal. Well, this age-old plant use works just as well in the woods as it does at the restaurant table. By learning to identify edible mint species (numerous plants in the genus *Mentha*) and using the leaves as a flavorful medicine, we can settle upset stomachs caused by bad food, illness, and overeating. Chew a few leaves or brew mint tea for relief.

4 RASH PREVENTION After coming into contact with poison ivy (or any of its relatives), washing with soap and water will help, but you can also try a traditional native plant remedy (which I have used successfully many times). Identify the plant jewelweed (*Impatiens capensis*), and crush the juicy, purplish-color stalk into a slimy paste. Briskly scrub this snotty-looking mush all over the skin that came into contact with poison ivy, poison oak, or poison sumac. After 2 minutes of contact, wash off the jewelweed mush with clean water. Using jewelweed within 30-45 minutes of exposure should result in little or no poison ivy reaction.

7 **BREWING INGREDIENTS**
You'll need a lot of sugar to create beer, wine, and other alcoholic beverages, and sugar can be hard to find in the wilderness. There are, however, a lot of wild plants that can be used as flavoring ingredients for your DIY adult drinks. Yarrow leaves (*Achillea millefolium*) can be used for infection control on wounds, but they can also provide a great flavor in beer, and they help to keep the bacteria level down in the fermenting beer liquid (giving the yeast plenty of room to grow). Other wild ingredients like spruce twig tips, edible fruits, and juicy blackberries can create some unique and appealing tastes in your wild brew.

8 **DENTAL CARE** The mouth is the gateway into the body, and dental issues can have far-reaching effects. In a survival situation, dental care is an often-overlooked priority. For cleaning your teeth, something as simple as a tuft of pine needles can make a passable toothbrush alternative. Just grab a small wad of these slender and prickly tree leaves, and scrub your teeth as best you can. For more serious issues, like a toothache, the astringent compound known as tannic acid can help to reduce swelling and pain. Crush and boil a handful of oak bark or fresh acorns in a cup of water, then use this tea-color water as a mouth rinse.

9 **SEDATIVE** Catnip (*Nepeta cataria*) can make your house cat bounce off the walls with high energy, but strangely enough, when the dried leaves of catnip are brewed as a tea, this beverage can have a calming effect for drinkers, similar to chamomile tea. This plant species is found worldwide, and its musky mint scent is quite distinctive. Combine 2 teaspoons (5 g) of dried catnip leaf with 8 ounces (240 ml) of very hot water. Steep, covered, for 15 minutes, and drink the tea right before bedtime.

10 **CANDLES** Wax Myrtle (*Morella cerifera*) is a common coastal shrub found across the southeastern U.S., from New Jersey to Texas. This shrub goes by another name, often associated with winter holidays: bayberry. These shrubs grow clusters of small, waxy berries, which can be processed into candle wax. For each pound of tiny berries you collect and boil in water, you'll be able to skim a little more than 1 ounce of fragrant wax from the surface of the water, which can then be turned into any candle form. Wax myrtle's fragrant leaves can also be crushed on the skin as a bug repellent, like pineapple weed leaves.

WILD BOAR AND GREEN CHILE STEW

SERVES 8

To my "working man's" palate, pork and green chiles are a match made in culinary heaven. The sharpness of the chiles and the rich unctuousness of the pork somehow balance and complement each other, without drowning out the other one. And when that pork has an even more intense flavor than usual (as feral hogs and wild boar will have), the green chiles are even more valuable—familiarizing the unfamiliar notes in the wild pork. Whether you hunted the boar with a spear in a primordial forest or you picked up a "Boston butt" at the corner market, don't be surprised if this dish goes into heavy rotation. Similarly, don't be surprised if the leftovers are few and far between.

- 1½ **pounds (700 g) fresh green chile peppers***
- 8 **ounces (230 g) tomatillos, husks removed and rinsed**
- 2 **tablespoons (30 ml) bacon grease, lard, or vegetable oil**
- 3½ **to 4 pounds (1.5 to 1.8 kg) wild boar shoulder, excess fat removed, cut into ½-inch pieces**
  Salt and black pepper
- 1 **large yellow onion, chopped**
- 6 **cloves garlic, minced**
- 1 **tablespoon (6 g) ground cumin**
- 1 **teaspoon (1 g) dried oregano**
- 2 **bay leaves**
- 2 **tablespoons (30 ml) cider vinegar**
- 4 **cups (1 l) chicken stock, plus more as needed**
- 1 **(16-ounce) (473-ml) can butter beans or other white beans, rinsed and drained**
  Hot cooked rice
  Chopped fresh cilantro (optional)

1. Turn oven to broil. Arrange peppers on a large foil-lined sheet pan. Broil peppers, turning occasionally, until charred on all sides, 15 to 20 minutes. Wrap peppers in foil in three or four bundles; set aside. When cool enough to handle, remove skins, stems, and seeds from peppers. Chop peppers.

2. Arrange tomatillos on the same sheet pan. Broil tomatillos until charred, turning once, 5 to 10 minutes. Chop tomatillos.

3. In a large Dutch oven heat bacon grease over high heat until sizzling. Pat meat dry with paper towels; season with salt and pepper. In three or four batches, cook meat until browned, 3 to 4 minutes. Using a slotted spoon, transfer meat to a large bowl.

4. Reduce heat to medium. Add the onion and cook until tender, 5 to 7 minutes. Add garlic, cumin, oregano, and bay leaves, and stir to combine. Add vinegar and increase heat to high, scraping up any browned bits from the bottom of the pot.

5. Add the meat, stock, peppers, and tomatillos. Bring to boiling; reduce heat. Simmer, covered, until meat is fork-tender, about 2 to 2½ hours.

6. Add beans to the stew. Cook until meat is tender, 30 to 40 minutes more. Season stew with salt and pepper to taste.

Serve over rice. Top with cilantro, if desired.

***Note:** You can use all one kind of a mild pepper—such as poblano or Anaheim—or a mix of mild and hot peppers, such as Hatch, serrano, or jalapeño.

EATING AFTER A CRISIS

After a major shakeup or calamity has taken place, the survivors will have more than a few responsibilities. In addition to the hard work of cleaning up, rebuilding, and recovering after the event, the "lucky ones" will have to care for themselves and others.

None of this will be as easy or convenient as it was before the disaster, and it's all going to be hard work. This toil will require energy, in two different forms: caloric energy for the human body, and some kind of heat energy for cooking. The energy that passes through our stomachs should come from good nutrition and provide plenty of calories. The energy to cook can come from a wide range of sources, as you'll see in the following pages. In this final chapter, we'll take a tour of the food topics and culinary skills you'd need to know when a fully functional kitchen isn't at your disposal. We'll take a look at water procurement and disinfection in a post-disaster setting, and the fire-building skills that will give you the heat to cook. You'll see how to build improvised ovens and other cooking contraptions, as well as some tips for scavenging food. As a grand finale, we'll share some of the weirdest and wildest recipes in the entire book (some of which should not be served to the faint of heart). Don't worry. These aren't just skills and information that would be applied in a post-nuclear, dystopian, apocalyptic, TEOTWAWKI (The End Of The World As We Know It) scenario. These skills and tips can be used in many other (less epic) situations. From feeding hungry folks as they evacuate during a fire-season burn to keeping your own strength up while cleaning out a flooded home, everyone has to eat to endure. We'll help you figure out how to make that happen in this final chapter, under almost any conditions.

119 TAKE STOCK OF YOUR SITUATION

Once the dust has settled after a disaster or an upheaval, it's time to take stock of your situation. Not only will you need to assess your current and future risks, you'll also need to determine what you have and what you need. Are there supplies that you merely wish you had? Or are there things that you truly need? Since human beings are terrible at predicting the future (and since each emergency situation is unique), there will always be things that you forget to stock in your emergency supplies. The first place to start is a very honest assessment of your wants and needs. Your kids may be screaming about cookies when they're hungry. That specific food is a "want." All they actually "need" are enough calories to stay healthy and active (and those can come from a food they don't like, just the same as the calories coming from cookies). So what do you actually "need" to survive? This supply set can include a well-stocked BOB (Bug Out Bag) for each family member, containing the basic survival supplies they'd need to subsist on their own for a short period. Items like food, first aid supplies, water, and sleeping bags are never bad ideas in these bags. Whether you're facing fire, flood, quakes, or an active hurricane season, it's also useful to fill some rugged plastic bins with additional supplies. These can come in handy when you're on the go or portaging to a survival camp. Antibacterial dish soap, toilet paper, hand sanitizer, and feminine hygiene products are needed for obvious reasons. A large cooking pot, metal spoons and bowls, dry goods (like rice, beans, flour, pasta, salt, and sugar) are game-changers when it comes to camp cooking. Round out your kit with a battery-powered lantern and spare batteries, first-aid kit, hatchet, camp saw, multitool, sharpening stone, radio with spare batteries, flashlight or headlamp with spare batteries, camp shovel, one box of gallon ziptop bags, three lighters, several bars of soap, manual can opener, kitchen knives and spoons, duct tape, trash bags, and a solar cell phone charger or battery backup. Just remember, when you're taking stock of your situation and supplies, keep asking yourself what you'll really need (and try to avoid obsessing over the things you merely want).

120 EMBRACE THE PLASTIC

A few extra tarps can serve as shelters, firewood coverings, rain ponchos, ground cloths, hammocks, and a host of other useful items. The more tarps you have, the better off your camp will be. The large trash bags in your gear list can also serve many functions. They can be used to create improvised rain gear and small tarps, and you can even fill them with leaves to make a DIY sleeping bag.

Perhaps the greatest use of these plastic panels is as a rain catch. Just a small amount of rain over several square feet can yield gallons of water. Hang up a tarp over your shelter, and you've also made a rain catch. Just set up the tarp on an angle, with a low spot on one side where the water will pour off. Set your bins and buckets under the lowest point of the tarp during the next rain shower.

121 CREATE ORDER WITH AREAS

The camp kitchen, tent sites, dishwashing area, latrine, and other critical camp features should be planned with safety and sanitation in mind (i.e. don't put the camp toilet next to the cooking area).

THE LATRINE Dig a latrine trench a good distance away from camp–and downwind. Leave the dirt that you dug up in a pile, and use a can as a scooper to cover up after each use. Keep some of your toilet paper handy in a waterproof ziptop bag. Maintain a little dignity and respect camp privacy by using a tarp to screen off the latrine area. If you cannot spare the tarp, then select a latrine area shielded by brush, big rocks, or other natural cover.

THE KITCHEN Set up your campfire cook pot using bricks, cinder blocks, rocks, or whatever else you have handy to create a safe and stable fireplace. Scrounge up a grill or an oven rack to make an even better cooking setup. The fireplace must be stable. If the pot falls over, a good amount of boiling water can scald anyone gathered around the fire.

THE WASHING AREA Dirty dishes can spread everything from dysentery to spinal meningitis; don't take shortcuts with camp cleanliness. Use a three-tub system–the first tub holds plain water to get the majority of food off the dishes, the second tub has a little dish soap to get the rest of the food off, and the third tub has a little bleach to rinse off the soap and disinfect the dishes. The final step is to air-dry the dishes in the sun.

122 MAKE CAMP LIFE EASIER

Add these elements to your camp for safety and efficiency.

CLINIC Have a designated area for your field hospital. You should select an area where the waterproof first-aid kit will reside and where wounds will be tended. This should not be near the kitchen area.

TRASH PIT Dig a hole for trash, but only if animals are not a local problem. If you have bears, feral dog packs, or other wild animals, then you'll have to shift strategies and burn all your garbage. Create a burn pit at least 100 yards (90 m) downwind of camp in an area that is not prone to wildfires.

FOOD STORAGE In areas with no bears and few scavengers, you can use one of your empty bins to serve as a food and cooking equipment storage locker. However, in bear country or areas with bold scavengers like rats and raccoons, you'll have to "bear bag" your food by hanging it up in a tree at least 15 feet (4.5 m) up and 100 yards (90 m) downwind from camp.

TOOLSHED You don't need to build an actual shed to make use of the tools you added to your supplies, but just make sure that your group keeps the multitools and duct tape in one spot so you can find them when you need them.

GREEN CHILE BUNKER STEW

SERVES 2

You don't need to have a secret underground bunker to dine like you're hiding in one. As unique as a fingerprint, each version of "bunker stew" can be as distinctive as the survivalist creating it. In its simplest form, bunker stew is a hearty soup created primarily from canned goods. By using foods preserved by canning, you'll have abundant moisture for the stew, and the dish will be ready to eat as soon as it is combined (and hopefully heated up for a few minutes to marry the flavors and provide a hot meal). Don't be shy with your natural creativity. It's your dish, so adding dried herbs and spices are your decision. It's also your call whether you add dry staple-food items to the pot (like rice or pasta). You'll need to cook the stew for an additional 20 to 30 minutes and probably add additional water if you incorporate dry goods, but items like rice can create a more filling dish. These additions can also bulk up the dish, allowing you to feed more people (but don't add dry beans; they'll take hours to cook and steal all of your moisture from the stew). There are four main components of this stew: a protein, a vegetable, a starch, and some seasoning. Play with these variables, and find your favorite combinations of canned goods. Don't feel trapped. You're allowed to use more than four cans of food as ingredients.

1   (12.5-ounce) (360 g) can chicken breast in water (protein)

1   (14.5-ounce) (420 g) can butter beans (both a starch and a vegetable)

1   small can of corn, approximately 8 ounces (160 g) (another starchy vegetable)

1   (4-ounce) (120 g) can mild green chiles (seasoning)

Salt, black pepper, dried herbs, and/or spices, to taste (optional)

1. Combine all four cans, undrained, in a medium saucepan over medium-high heat. Bring to boiling; reduce heat to medium-low. Simmer, uncovered, for 10 to 15 minutes, breaking up the chicken chunks. Stir in additional seasonings to taste. (I like to add a small amount of garlic salt—the chicken is already quite salty—and plenty of freshly ground black pepper to add freshness.)

DON'T GET TOO BRAVE WITH YOUR LONG-STORED CANNED GOODS. ALTHOUGH CANNED FOOD CAN LAST YEARS BEYOND THE "BEST BY" DATE, DON'T USE ANY CANS THAT ARE SWOLLEN, LEAKING, OR "BLOW OUTWARD". WHEN THE CAN OPENER PIERCES THEM.

123 KNOW YOUR WATER

Safe drinking water can make or break an emergency situation. Contrary to what you see on many survival shows, it's never wise to drink raw water from sources in the wild. Numerous pathogens and contaminants can taint the water supply wherever you are and cause serious harm or death if consumed without the right treatment or disinfecting process. Consider these methods to deal with suspected problems.

PROBLEM	EFFECT	ZONE	METHOD
Bacteria & Viruses	These can cause diarrhea, vomiting, dysentery, and death	Freshwater anywhere, especially in the tropics	Boiling, chemical disinfection, UV devices, and water filters
Protozoa	These can cause diarrhea, dysentery, and death	Freshwater anywhere	Boiling, chemical disinfection, and water filters
Parasites	Fluke worms and other parasites can cause liver damage, lung ailments, and a host of odd symptoms that are potentially fatal	Freshwater anywhere	Boiling, chemical disinfection, and water filters
Salt	Even drinking a small amount of saltwater can lead to kidney damage and electrolyte imbalance, which can be fatal	Oceans and bays	Steam distillation and reverse osmosis filtering will remove salt from water
Heavy metals	Depending on the type of contamination and its severity, heavy metals like lead and mercury can cause organ damage and death	Rivers and oceans near industrial areas	Steam distillation will remove all heavy metals from water
Radiation	A variety of cancers and tissue damage occurs from ingesting irradiated water, leading to a long and painful death	Freshwater and saltwater after a radiological event	Steam distillation is the most effective method to remove radiation, but it is not 100 percent effective

124 DISTILL WATER WITH A CANNER

Radiation, lead, salt, heavy metals, and several other contaminants could taint your water supply after a disaster, and if you try to filter them out, you will ruin your expensive water filter. In a scenario where the only water available is dangerous water, there aren't many options to work with. The safest solution lies in water distillation. Water can be heated into steam, and the steam can then be captured to create pure water–removing many forms of contamination, including radioactive fallout. Distillation won't get out all possible contaminants, such as volatile oils and certain organic compounds, but it will work on most heavy particles.

A quick way to make a steam distiller is by using a pressure canner and a length of small-diameter copper tubing. The best part of this operation (aside from getting safe water) is that the canner stays intact. This allows you to shift gears from water distillation to food preservation very easily (assuming you are not dealing with radiation). The only tricky part is getting the copper line fitted to the steam vent on the canner's lid.

SET UP Locate a canner and about 4 feet (1.2 m) of ¼-inch (6-mm) copper line. Set your canner pot on your stove top, over a camping stove, or over an improvised cinder block fireplace. Fill your canner pot two-thirds full with questionable water and screw on the canner lid. This can be saltwater or muddy water–any water except that tainted by fuels (which evaporate at low temps).

CREATE YOUR COIL The coil, also known as the worm, is made from copper line coiled in a downward spiral.

Use a stick or some other support for the coil to avoid stress on the joint at the canner's steam vent. Ream out one end of the copper tubing and force it down over the steam fitting on top of the canner lid if it's smaller than the steam vent. Compress the line if it's bigger than the vent. Tie this joint with rags or dope it with a paste of flour and water once everything is in position.

LIGHT IT UP Whether a stove or a campfire powers your still, you'll have to play with the size of the fire for best results. If you run it too hot, you'll just blow steam out of the coil. If you run it too cool, nothing will happen. Start out with a small amount of heat, and work your way up if needed. Once the pot gets close to boiling, water should start to pour out of the coil. The surrounding air will naturally cool the copper, and the steam will condense into distilled, drinkable water.

125 BOIL IN A BOTTLE

Did you know that you can use your water bottle to boil water by the campfire? It's a great backup method for disinfecting your drinking water. Many water bottles developed for the outdoor-sports industry are made from impact-resistant and heat-resistant Lexan plastic. While you shouldn't try to put your Lexan bottle over a fire,

you can put the heat of a fire inside the bottle using hot stones.

STEP 1 Collect about two dozen small stones from a dry location.

STEP 2 Heat the stones in your fire for 30 minutes, and use some wooden tongs to drop a hot stone in the bottle of water.

STEP 3 Replace each stone as it cools. The stones will emit heat into the water, bringing it to a boil. It will keep boiling if you keep replacing the stones. Keep one stone at a time in the water until 10 minutes have passed.

POWER-OUTAGE PIZZA

SERVES 2

Maybe a bad summer storm knocked out your power for a day, or a gargantuan solar flare wiped out the entire electrical grid—in any case, you're craving pizza and the oven is out cold. Fire up the grill and cook your pie on it. Not only does it work just as well as the oven, you get great smoky flavor too. Or, if you have a frozen pizza in your rapidly thawing freezer, you can toss that on the grill as well. Now the average frozen pizza is carefully designed to be beginner friendly, but it's also designed to be baked in a modern home oven at a specific temperature for a certain length of time. All those details go out the window when you're forced to improvise a method of cooking your pizza while the utilities are out. Don't give up! With a little ingenuity, you'll get that pizza either way and be glad to eat.

FOR THE CRUST:

1	(0.25–ounce) (7 g) package active yeast
1	cup (240 ml) warm water
¼	teaspoon (1 g) sugar
3½	cups (840 ml) all-purpose flour
2	teaspoons (10 ml) olive oil, plus more for the bowl
1	teaspoon (5 g) sea salt
1	teaspoon (2.5 g) Italian seasoning
½	teaspoon (3 g) garlic powder

FOR THE PIZZA:

½	cup (120 ml) marinara or pizza sauce
1	cup (200 g) sliced wild game sausage
1	cup (80 g) shredded mozzarella cheese
1	cup shredded Fontina cheese

1. Make the crust: Mix yeast with the water and add sugar; allow to sit 15 minutes or until foamy. In a large bowl stir together flour, oil, salt, Italian seasoning, and garlic powder until combined and a dough ball forms. On a lightly floured surface, knead dough until smooth. Place dough in a lightly oiled bowl; turn to coat dough. Cover with plastic wrap and let rise 1 hour. Punch dough down and return to the bowl to rise 1 hour. Divide dough into 2 balls. Roll or pat dough into 2 crusts about ¼– inch (6 mm) thick.

2. Make the pizza: Preheat a grill for medium-high heat. Place crusts on oiled grates and grill just long enough to create grill marks and stiffen the dough, about 1 minute. Turn crusts over; divide sauce, sausage, and cheeses each crust. Grill until cheese is melted, 5 to 8 minutes. Cool slightly before cutting into slices.

FILL EMPTY BELLIES AND CALM FRAZZLED NERVES DURING A POWER OUTAGE WITH ONE OF THE WORLD'S MOST POPULAR FOODS—PIZZA!

126 SCAVENGE FOR FOOD

If you've got a fully-stocked food pantry and a functional kitchen in the wake of a disaster, count yourself among the fortunate ones. Not everyone will have that, or even the ability to get prepared for a disaster ahead of time. And sometimes even the best-prepared people can have a patch of bad luck, losing the supplies that were supposed to get them through a crisis. When the brown stuff hits the fan and you're caught without enough food, it may be time to salvage, search, and scavenge for foods. These are ancient skills, likely predating hunter-gatherer cultures, but there are plenty of modern issues that would have boggled our ancestors. With the preservatives and packaging of today, it may not be clear whether a food is good or bad. Maybe you're looking for foodstuffs in the storeroom of a burnt-out grocery store. Say "yes" to

the canned and dry goods. Say "no" to the ballooning cartons of OJ and milk. For those who aren't too proud to go Dumpster-diving, you may be able to grab some recently expired baked goods in bags or boxes, wilted fruits and veggies, or other potentially salvageable food. Trust your eyes and especially your nose for this work. When foods don't look right, that's a little red flag. When foods don't smell right, that's a big red flag. Yes, you may be very hungry, but tainted food could put you in a worse situation than you're already fighting. Food-borne bacteria and other organisms can lead to significant illness (and it's a little hard to digest any food when you're puking your guts out or camped out on the toilet seat). As with most issues in the realm of survival, it's better to be safe than sorry (even if "safe" leaves you hungry).

TIM'S TOP 10

127 SURVIVAL BRIBES FOR KIDS

Children and youth need to be taught survival skills just as much as anyone else, but at the end of the day, they're still kids. Sometimes it helps to offer incentive, or just something as a comfort, for a kid in a stressful situation, especially when it comes to disasters. Consider adding these snacks, sweets, and trinkets as "bribes" in your survival stash.

1 HARD CANDY This doesn't have to be the old-fashioned hard candy that your grandma left on the coffee table in an open dish for guests. This can be your classic candy or contemporary favorites. These treats should be mostly sugar, which enables them to last for long periods of time. Think Jolly Ranchers and Lifesavers, not chocolate (since the fat will eventually go rancid).

2 CRAYONS If you can spare a bit of scrap paper, a box of crayons can provide hours of artwork fun (for kids of all ages). These are a great accompaniment for the next item, coloring books.

3 ACTIVITY BOOKS If you know your audience, the right activity and coloring books can be a great reward for a job well done, and an excellent distraction from the troubles at hand.

4 KID'S LITERATURE A good storybook can transport us to a faraway place and time, which could be desirable if the present place and time are terrible. Choose from the most popular children's literature titles of all time, or get your kiddo a book about their favorite modern characters. Keep this collection updated, if you choose something modern, since kids often change their preferences and lose interest in things they formerly adored.

5 CHEWING GUM This treat can freshen someone's breath and help take the edge off of hunger. Your child's favorite gum could keep them in good spirits.

6 SMALL TOYS Simple little toys can offer quite the boost to little ones who are struggling. I'd recommend small stuffed animals. These don't require batteries or make any noise, plus they are huggable, comforting, and easy to transport (since most are very lightweight).

7 SNACK MIXES Even though Twinkies may have enough preservatives to outlast a nuclear winter, most snacks don't have a long shelf life (making them unsuitable for long-term storage). Certain snack mixes, however, may be available for the long haul. Survival food storage companies offer canned cookie and pudding mixes, rated for multi-year shelf life. Just make sure you have all the shelf-stable ingredients to complete each recipe (things like egg replacer and powdered milk can be vital in the preparation of these snacks).

8 CRAFT SUPPLIES Another time-consumer, crafts supplies can be anything that you think your kids would enjoy. Colorful string can be used for weaving friendship bracelets. A few beads can make even fancier jewelry. Construction paper and glue can make all kinds of projects. Pick things your kids will like, and look like a hero when you roll them out during low morale.

9 JOURNAL For those kids who have a hard time expressing their thoughts and feelings, a journal may give them a much-needed outlet in tough times. This journal could even become a valuable record of your family's ordeal (think: *The Diary of Anne Frank*).

10 THEIR OWN SURVIVAL GEAR For older and more responsible children, giving them their own survival kit or supplies can be very empowering.

TUNA COOKED IN ITS OWN OIL

SERVES 1-2

As canned protein goes, a tin of tuna fish can be more utilitarian than desirable. You'll eat it because you're hungry or because you want to build some muscle, but most people won't get excited about it. In fact, most people will require some major modifications to actually enjoy their tuna. Tuna Noodle Casserole (see recipe #2) is a great option, if you have a working oven and lots of other ingredients. Without the oven but using lots of additions, we can convert those flavorless fish flakes into a tuna salad sandwich. But what can you do to the tuna when you don't have all the extras and appliances? If the tuna is packed in oil, you can cause a major transformation of taste with this off-the-grid tuna cooking hack.

1   (5- to 12-ounce) (145–350 g) can tuna packed in oil
1   paper napkin
    Matches or lighter

1. Open the can, leaving the oil in place. Set the can in a fireproof location, such as a concrete surface or stone slab.

2. Place one layer of paper napkin over the tuna, pressing it down tight against the contents of the can.

3. Light the edge of the paper napkin with a match or lighter. The flames will spread across the surface of the container over the next few minutes, and the burning paper will act as a wick, burning the oil and conducting heat downward into the can. This may burn for 10 minutes or longer, depending on the amount of oil in the can.

4. When the flame has gone out on its own, pick away any bits of charred napkin and enjoy the warm tuna with roasted flavor.

IF EVERY BITE OF FOOD COUNTS IN A LONG-TERM CRISIS, BURNING THE TUNA OIL TO TRANSFORM THE FLAVOR IS A TERRIBLE WASTE OF CALORIES. YOU'D BE BETTER OFF MIXING THE TUNA AND EVERY DROP OF OIL INTO A FOOD THAT CAN BE SHARED WITH THE GROUP.

128 COOK ON A CAMP STOVE

For those who already have a camping stove and are familiar with its use, firing up the cooker during a utility outage will be familiar and easy. Camping stoves come in a wide range of sizes and styles, with various features and fuel requirements. Some burn small propane bottles, while others use liquid fuels. Do your research. Find the best choice for your needs, and consider which fuels will be readily available in a crisis. Maybe you only need a small one-burner stove to boil water and heat up a few cans of soup. Or if you're cooking for a crowd, a multiburner stove may be just the thing you need. Plan ahead by getting any accessories that make sense, such as adapters that allow you to use different sizes of fuel tanks or accompaniments that make the stove easier to use.

129 HEAT UP WITH CHEMISTRY

Sometimes it's not practical or safe to heat food with a flame-based cooking method. If there's any chance of a gas leak or if you're stuck indoors in tight quarters, fire just isn't reasonable. Thankfully, there's an alternative. The flameless heater pouch (commonly seen in military MREs) is able to harness a safe natural phenomenon: chemically created heat. When iron rusts, iron atoms combine with oxygen to create iron oxide. This oxidation process actually gives off heat, though it's very slow under normal circumstances. When magnesium dust, salt, and a little iron dust are combined, adding water creates a very fast oxidation process (and a lot of heat). In just a few seconds, the flameless heater reaches the boiling point. To use the heater, add the directed amount of water and insert a pouch or can of food into the bag. Quickly close the bag and allow it to steam for 10 minutes. Once heated, your meal is ready!

130 UNDERSTAND YOUR FUEL TYPES

You'll probably want to have a range of fuel options on hand, depending on your needs and what sort of emergency you feel is most likely to happen in your region. This chart gives you a starting point for considering your needs and making decisions.

FUEL	SOLIDS			LIQUIDS				GASES
	WOOD	COAL	CHARCOAL	PETROL	DIESEL	KEROSENE	OIL	NATURAL GAS PROPANE / BUTANE
COOKING	●	●	●			●		●
HEATING	●	●	●			●	●	●
LIGHTING	●					●	●	●
ELECTRICITY (GENERATORS)				●	●			●
VEHICLES				●	●			
STORAGE	Dry storage (bins, bags)			Plastic or metal canisters/jugs				Pressurized bottles/tanks
PROS	• Durable (if kept dry) • Usable indoors- and outdoors (campfires, stoves, fireplaces, etc.)			• Portable • Versatile (some stoves, lamps, generators, etc. will accept multiple liquid fuels)				• Most versatile fuel type
CONS	• Charcoal can only be used to cook outdoors • Can be heavy • Requires a lot of storage space • Will not burn if wet • Wood can rot			• Some liquid fuels can degrade over time (unusable for vehicles) or evaporate/leak • Vapors are flammable				• Sealed bottles or tanks require refills • Can be punctured • Portable only in small to moderate amounts

131 STORE FUEL RIGHT

No matter how much liquid fuel you're planning to stockpile, certain considerations remain the same. You're dealing with a combustible, poisonous material, so you should apply a few extra measures of caution.

CONTAINERS Even the fumes are combustible, so liquid fuel should be stored in airtight containers that do not vent. You should be able to walk into the area where your fuel is stored and smell nothing. If that's not the case, either fumes or liquid is leaking, and you need to fix that fast. Store your fuel in approved plastic or metal containers, and check them frequently.

LOCATION Don't store fuel in your basement or even in your garage if you can help it. The ideal spot is a storage shed on your property located at least 30 feet (9 m) from your home (this is true for firewood as well). In the event of a house fire, you don't want to add any more combustibles to the mix. Some recommend underground tanks, but this is illegal in many places and a serious risk to the quality of your groundwater. Don't risk it. If you want to stockpile fuel in bulk, you can purchase above-ground storage drums.

TEMPERATURE As with food storage, you want your fuel kept somewhere clean, dark, and as cold as possible. Direct light and higher temperatures can degrade fuel's quality quickly and, in a worst-case scenario, pose a fire risk as well.

CAMP STOVE RAMEN

SERVES 2

Fire up your camp stove! There's ramen to cook. This ubiquitous noodle isn't just a staple food of college students and those living on a budget. Ramen can be very tasty and very filling when prepared well. In the event that your normal home kitchen isn't open for business, consider this simple recipe for ramen noodles prepared on a camping stove. You might be surprised how much you like it.

1   to 1½ cups (240 to 360 ml) cold water

5½ to 6 cups (1.3 to 1.4 l) water

2   large eggs

2   (3-ounce) (90 g) packages beef flavor instant ramen

4   ounces (120 g) beef jerky, coarsely shredded

1   jalapeño, seeded if desired and sliced

1   medium carrot, cut into matchsticks

¼   of a small red onion, sliced

4   mushrooms, sliced

    Fresh cilantro leaves

1   lime, halved

1. Place the cold water in a medium bowl. In a medium saucepan or pot bring 5½ to 6 cups (1.3 to 1.4 l) water to boiling on a camp stove over high heat. Add whole eggs to boiling water; reduce heat to medium-low and cook for 6 minutes. Carefully transfer eggs to the cold water.

2. Return hot water to the camp stove over medium-low heat. Add the ramen seasoning packets and beef jerky to the hot water. Cook for 2 minutes or until beef is softened. Add the ramen noodles and cook 1 minute. Add jalapeño, carrot, onion, and mushrooms, and cook 1 minute or until noodles are softened. Divide ramen between two bowls; top with cilantro and squeeze lime juice over top.

3. Peel eggs when thoroughly cooled. Using a small knife or a length of clean fishing line, cut eggs in half and add to ramen. (Yolks will be runny.)

COLLEGE KIDS SURVIVE ON THIS STUFF, AND SO CAN YOU. RAMEN NOODLES HAVE A HIGHER FAT CONTENT THAN MOST OTHER NOODLES WHEN COMPARED DRY. OUNCE FOR OUNCE, MORE FAT MEANS MORE CALORIES.

132 GET MORE LIGHT

Having already mentioned three different light sources you should carry, it only seems natural to mention three ignition sources to bring. Why three? By carrying three, you have one to lose, one to break, and one to use.

BUTANE LIGHTERS These modern marvels can light more fires that a huge box of matches. Just store them in some way that doesn't press the button, which would cause all the butane to escape.

MATCHES Each match acts like a little piece of kindling, helping the baby fire to burn. They also provide an open flame like the lighter, though most matches aren't that reliable when moisture is an issue.

SPARK RODS Ferrocerium rods can throw a lot of sparks, but that's their problem. Not every tinder is able to light from sparks; some requires an open flame. Still, a spark rod can be a useful backup to matches or lighters.

133 MAKE CHAR CLOTH

For easier fire starting, a great resource you can make is char cloth. This is the same "char" that you'd use for traditional flint-and-steel fire starting, and it's easy to make. Get a small metal box, like a candy tin, and poke one small hole in it. Fill the can with scraps of dry cotton or linen cloth, fluffy plant-based tinder, cotton balls or crumbly rotten wood. Chuck the can into a campfire and let it cook for about 5 minutes or until smoke stops jetting out of the vent. Use a stick to roll the can out of the fire, cover the pin hole, and allow it to cool before opening. The contents should have become brittle and black, and shrunken in size. If properly burned (long enough but not too long), it will be excellent at catching sparks from ferrocerium rods, flint and steel, and optical methods.

134 USE A BATTERY

The same battery that can be a source of light can also be used with jumper cables and tinder to start a fire.

MAKE SPARKS FLY Carefully clamp your jumper cables to the positive and negative terminals on the vehicle battery. Then touch the metal jaws of the free ends of the cables together. For best results, make this contact over a nest of fluffy tinder material that is sitting on the ground.

STAY SAFE Don't clamp or hold the jaws together, as this can create a closed circuit and heat up the battery to a dangerous level—acidic explosion, anyone? Just sweep the jaws past each other, touching them as they pass. The shower of molten metal sparks that will result from this contact will be intense and startling, so wear gloves and goggles if you have them.

TRY AN ALTERNATIVE If this is too scary, sharpen both ends of a pencil and clamp the jumper cables to each end; in mere moments, the pencil will burst into flame.

135 BRING A FRESNEL LENS

There's only one way I know to level the playing field in an emergency: redundancy. And while we've mentioned bringing three fire starters to the party, why not carry one more? The Fresnel lens is a small, thin plastic magnifying "glass" that can tuck right into your wallet. Use it just as you would use a standard magnifying glass to make fire. Focus a blinding pinpoint of sunlight on the flat spot in some dark tinder, angling the lens to make the dot of light as small and round as possible. Manipulate the lens at different angles and at different distances from the tinder until you have the perfect dot, and the smoke should start to flow from this hot spot immediately. Blow gently across the tinder while you are magnifying light on it. Your extra oxygen and air movement will cause burning fibers to spread their ignited red glow.

MAGNIFIER + RULER + FIRE STARTER

FRESNEL LENS

136 PASS THE CHIPS

Snack chips are delicious and packed with calories, and it's the reason they are calorie-dense that allows them to become amazing fire starters. Unless they are some kind of healthy chip, they are made with a generous amount of oil (most chips being fried in fat). This means that we can use these greasy chips for a phenomenal fire starter. Just apply an open flame to the edge of a chip and hold it for a few seconds. As the grease begins to vaporize, the chip begins to burn like a torch. Add this chip and a few more to your fire lay for a campfire, or use them to light your charcoal for a grid-down barbecue. And the best part is that they don't even have to be fresh! This is a great use for the old rancid chips you found while scavenging for food in the back of your pantry.

SMOKEY MOUNTAINS BRUNSWICK STEW

SERVES 4 TO 6

There's a little feud going on when it comes to the origin of Brunswick stew. Both Brunswick County (in my home state of Virginia) and the city of Brunswick, Georgia, make the claim that they were the birthplace of this flavorful stew. In the Virginia version of the story, some hungry hunters got a squirrel in the woods of Brunswick County. To make the meat go farther, they stewed the meat with corn and beans, thickening the broth with little bits of stale bread. This recipe (minus the bread) certainly predates these hunters, and the naming of Brunswick County, as these indigenous ingredients have been used to make stew for centuries in the New World. And whether you land a "tree rat," a real rat, or some chicken, this satisfying stew will certainly feed the hungry hunters in your survival camp.

3	squirrels, skinned and washed
5½	cups (1.3 l) vegetable broth, divided
2	tablespoons (30 g) butter
1	medium red onion, chopped
3	red new potatoes, diced
1	cup (190 g) lima beans
1	cup (100 g) okra
1	cup (170 g) corn kernels
1	(14.5–ounce) (428 ml) can diced tomatoes
¾	cup (180 ml) Classic BBQ Sauce (see recipe #40) or purchased barbecue sauce
1	tablespoon (15 ml) Worcestershire sauce
1	tablespoon (15 ml) sorghum molasses
1	teaspoon (5 g) kosher salt
½	teaspoon (1 g) black pepper
¼	teaspoon (1 g) cayenne pepper
	Corn bread (optional)
	Coleslaw (optional)

1. In a large stockpot bring the squirrels and 2½ cups (600 ml) broth to boil over medium-high heat. Reduce heat to low. Simmer, covered, for 30 minutes. Remove squirrels. When cool enough to handle, remove meat from bones.

2. Meanwhile, in a large saucepan melt butter over medium heat. Add onions and cook just until browned, about 5 minutes. Add remaining 3 cups (720 ml) broth, potatoes, lima beans, okra, corn, and tomatoes. Bring to boiling; reduce heat and simmer, stirring occasionally, until vegetables are tender, about 15 minutes. Add barbecue sauce, Worcestershire sauce, molasses, salt, black pepper, cayenne pepper, and squirrel meat. Simmer for 10 minutes. Serve with corn bread and coleslaw, if desired.

IF YOU'RE OUT OF BBQ SAUCE AND DON'T HAVE THE INGREDIENTS TO MAKE IT, TRY A DIFFERENT SAUCE IN YOUR BRUNSWICK STEW. HEINZE 57 SAUCE IS A POPULAR CHOICE, OR TRY EQUAL AMOUNTS OF KETCHUP AND MUSTARD.

137 TRY A WAX STOVE

A shallow metal can (like one for tuna, or lozenges, or mints), some wax, and a few strips of cardboard can turn into a quick cookstove with a long burn time. Just follow these easy steps.

STEP 1 Fill the can with coiled strips of cardboard, packing it as tightly as possible.

STEP 2 Pour in melted wax (any kind will work, but beeswax is best). Be careful when handling the hot wax, and don't completely drown the cardboard under wax. A little bit of cardboard should be sticking up as a wick for easy lighting.

STEP 3 You can light it now with a match and watch your stove flame up, or let it cool to use later.

STEP 4 Set up bricks or rocks around the stove to set your cookware above the flames. Use a flat item, like tin foil, to extinguish the stove if your cooking is done before you run out of fuel.

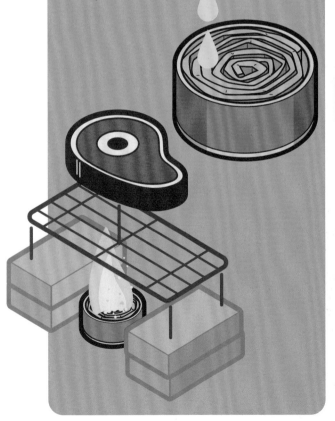

138 BUILD A BLOCK ROCKET

If you've got wood to burn, and you can source some cinder blocks in the rubble, you can build a cinder block rocket stove in just a few minutes!

STEP 1 Find three standard cinder blocks, each with two holes. A fourth "block" can be pieced together from cinder block caps and bricks, or you can use a hammer to knock the ends out of a fourth standard block. If you're lucky, you might even find an "H" shaped block that is ready to go.

STEP 2 Fit the blocks together as shown. One will go on the bottom, with the "H" shaped section above it. A side block allows fuel and air to enter, and a top block provides a chimney effect.

STEP 3 Add a crushed tin can for a fuel rest and air intake, and some kind of grate over the top hole to set pots upon (without sealing off the chimney). Light your block rocket with some dry sticks and crumpled paper.

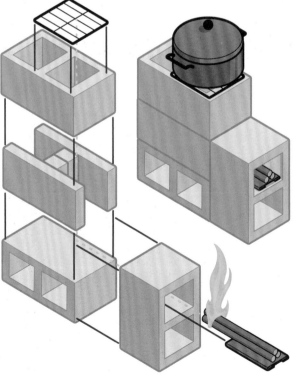

139 FIRE UP A ROCKET STOVE

Long beloved of backpackers and campers, this insulated stove makes lots of heat from small pieces of wood and lets you boil water or cook food without any need of electricity or gas. You can make one using just a few 12-ounce (355-ml) soup cans, a large coffee can or empty paint can, and some all-natural kitty litter with no preservatives.

STEP 1 Cut the top and bottom off one soup can to make a feeder tube. Then, cut the top from another soup can to make your burning chamber. Lastly, cut the bottom and top off of a third can, and use tin snips to cut it open.

STEP 2 Trace the feeder tube's circumference onto the chamber's side. Cut out the circle. Do the same with your coffee or paint can. Insert your feeder tube through the larger outer can and into the burning chamber inside it.

STEP 3 Roll up the third soup can, and slide it about half an inch (1.25 cm) into the top of the burning chamber. Fill the remaining space inside the large can with kitty litter.

STEP 4 Place a cook surface (such as a cast-iron burner top from a junked stove) on top of the large can. Put small sticks into the tube and light them with a long match or fireplace lighter. Keep feeding sticks in to keep the heat high. (Note: The first time you light the stove, do so without cooking over it—many commercial cans have a toxic coating that should be burned off before using the unit.)

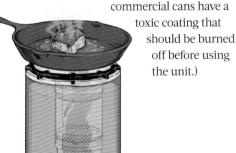

140 BUILD A PENNY STOVE

Strong alcohol is a common and environmentally friendly fuel that you can use with complex or simple cookstoves, but it doesn't get much simpler than a penny stove. Here's how to make one.

STEP 1 Gather two aluminum cans, tin snips, a hammer, a nail, a small coin like a penny, and high-proof alcohol.

STEP 2 Cut around the bottom of each can with tin snips, 1½ inches (4 cm) from the end. Crimp the cut edge of one piece, and force the crimped one inside the other.

STEP 3 Use the hammer and nail to punch a dozen holes around the top perimeter and several holes in the center of the top.

STEP 4 Pour your alcohol in the center holes, but not so full that it spills. Denatured alcohol is great, 90% isopropyl alcohol is marginal, and anything less won't work well. Set it on a steady fire-proof spot and light it. Cover the center hole with the coin and suspend your cookpot over the burning stove.

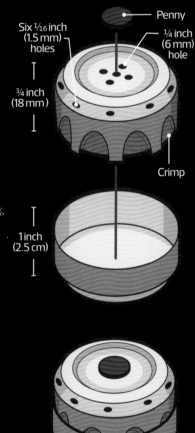

Penny

Six ¹⁄₁₆ inch (1.5 mm) holes

¼ inch (6 mm) hole

¾ inch (18 mm)

Crimp

1 inch (2.5 cm)

SQUAB BAKED IN A TIN-CAN OVEN

SERVES 1

Large metal cans don't have to be tossed in the trash when you've emptied them. As you will see in item 139, there have long been many survival uses for empty cans—which were once made from tin but are now made from aluminum. If you're lucky enough to have the wood to make a fire, a large empty can, and something to cook, you can create a handy little metal oven that is heated with hot coals. This particular can-cooking trick of "squab in a can" was shown to me by my good friend Rick Hueston during one of my primitive cooking classes. The results were impressive, and the tiny chicken he cooked was delicious! Here's how you can replicate this simple yet excellent cooking experience.

1   **Cornish game hen or a similar-size bird**

1   **#10 steel can, empty with one end removed**

     Aluminum foil

     Wood stake

1. Light a fire and begin burning hardwoods to create long-lasting coals. As the coals are forming, find a thick wood stake that is about 1 foot long. (It can be deadwood or nontoxic green wood.) Drive the stake into the ground near the fire, deep enough for stability but tall enough to keep the bottom of the can from touching the ground.

2. Place foil on the ground around the base of the stake, then place the bird on the stake with its feet touching the ground. Cover the bird with the can, adjusting can over bird so open end of can fits tightly to the ground. Using a small shovel, place a ring of burning coals around the base of the can, and pile some hot coals on top of the can.

3. Add fresh coals as they burn down, about every 15 to 20 minutes. Cook the bird for 1½ hours, then start to check for doneness. When the meat is falling off the bone, it's done.

Safety note: If your large can has an obvious or suspected plastic coating, burn the can in a fire prior to using it.

IF THE BIRD IS DONE AND YOU HAVE SOME BREAD DOUGH, THE SAME SETUP CAN BE USED (WITH ADDITIONAL COALS) TO MAKE BREAD ON A STICK.

10 SURVIVAL USES FOR
SARDINES

1 EMERGENCY PET FOOD Just because sardines in a can are intended for human consumption, this doesn't mean that our four-legged friends can't enjoy them too. Cats and dogs could subsist for quite a while on sardines, if no other pet food sources are available. While sardines packed in oil would be a little rich (and too calorie-dense) for a complete dog diet, fat-eating felines will do well feasting on this high-calorie snack (in moderation). Sardines packed in water would be a better dog food. Some of your other pets may even be able to eat this fishy food in a pinch (ask your vet at your pet's next checkup to be sure).

2 FISH OIL CANDLE The oil used for sardine packing is rarely pure fish oil, but after bathing these little fish in its greasy goodness, the oil from a sardine will take on a decidedly fishy aroma. If you can stomach this as a candle scent (there's a good reason that candle shops don't sell fish-scented tapers), you can turn this into an odd but effective light source. Once you've enjoyed (or not enjoyed) eating the sardines, leave the oil in the metal can. Lay a small bit of natural plant fiber cord in the pool of oil and light the end of the cord with a flame. This makeshift candle will give a surprising amount of light until the oil burns out.

3 SIGNAL MIRROR The flash of sunlight from a signal mirror can be seen up to 10 miles (16 km) away, making it a valuable piece of gear in an outdoor emergency. The shiny interior (or exterior) of a sardine can is able to do this, especially if you have a way to polish it. Try rubbing the metal with a little chocolate or some kind of "low grit" toothpaste for a few hours (that's not a typo, we said "*hours*" of rubbing) with a piece of paper or a rag. Yes, this could take a while but if it means getting the attention of an aircraft or boat that could rescue you, isn't it worth it? Besides, you've got nothing but time on your hands in most outdoor survival situations.

4 CAMP STOVE If you have a little high-proof alcohol you can spare, and an empty sardine can, you can combine these seemingly incompatible items to produce a simple camp stove for an improvised cooking rig. This booze should be very high proof liquor. A splash of wine won't do it (the alcohol-by-volume is too low). If you are short on moonshine, then coil up some cardboard strips in the can and drizzle melted wax over the strips. This becomes a "fire can," which can be used for cooking, lighting, or emergency fire starting. If wax isn't available, you could even use the sardine oil and cardboard strips as your DIY camp stove.

5 TRAP BAIT Raccoons and some other game animals love fishy-scented things. This means a dribble of sardine liquid or a few actual sardine pieces can act as a powerful lure to draw these omnivores to your traps. It is an investment, to give up some calories in the hope of gaining more calories. But that raccoon or bobcat that trips your trap will give you a warm and beautiful fur, and it could be a welcome change of menu (if times get tough). Just keep in mind that raccoons and rabies go hand in hand, so use due caution when skinning your quarry, and cook all wild game meat (especially common disease carriers) until well done.

6 SURVIVAL KIT In your search for self-reliance gear, you may have encountered certain "sardine can" survival kits that are commercially available. These are kits full of survival supplies, packaged in pull-top sardine cans. While the idea of a waterproof container is a good concept, the contents of these kits are sometimes sub-par. For better results (when your life is on the line), fill a clean and empty sardine can with good survival gear, then use a generous amount of duct tape to seal it up. Now you have a water-resistant can, quality survival goodies, and some duct tape (good for a thousand and one survival uses)!

7 SARDINE SEASONINGS
Maybe you're sitting on a bunker full of these stinky little canned fish. Or maybe you just have a can or two in the pantry. Both the oil and the fish can provide an interesting flavor to many other foods, and they can provide an unexpected pop in many meals (survival dining or otherwise). Drizzle the sardine can oil onto a bowl of wild greens for a survival salad dressing. Use the sardines themselves in sauces and dips. A little bit of sardine goodness can go a long way, so use this fish seasoning sparingly. You can always add more sardine oil or chunks, but it's a lot harder to take that strong flavor out of a dish!

8 MINI FRYING PAN The first frying pans are at least 3,000 years old, made from copper in ancient Mesopotamia. Greeks and Romans later developed their own flat-bottomed pans, similar to the pans of today. A wide range of frying, baking, and boiling tasks can be accomplished with frying pans, and the largest sardine cans make a fine little frying pan for a one-person backpacking cook set. You could even boil water in this shallow container, though it would take a while to get any reasonable volume to drink. By carefully opening the can, the lid can be left attached as a temporary frying pan handle (though it will eventually break).

9 SHELTER SMOKER A shelter smoker isn't complicated, but it can be a major asset in buggy areas. If you have a bug-infested shack, shed, or hut that you need to smoke out, you can chase away the insects with the combined efforts of a fire, a large empty sardine can, and some rotten wood. Simply transfer some red-hot coals from your fire into the sardine can, which serves as a great fire-proof smoking tray. Crumble some dry rotten wood over the coals, and place the container in a fire-proof spot in the shelter. The can full of coals and wood will create tons of smoke, and should resolve your bug troubles, at least temporarily.

10 PEOPLE FOOD Just as certain pets can eat sardines, you can eat them too. The global standard for canned sardines includes over a dozen fish species that may be classed as sardines. Whichever kind you end up with, a few crackers and hot sauce will work wonders to liven up these long-dead herring cousins. These small creatures are rich in marine omega-3 fatty acids, touted to reduce your risk of cardiovascular ailments, and potentially even reduce your chances of developing Alzheimer's disease. Sardines are also a great way to get vitamin D, calcium, vitamin B12, and protein into your diet. Some folks even like them!

SOLAR OVEN BROWNIES

SERVES 12

Solar ovens are an increasingly popular cooking method, presenting an interesting alternative for slow cooking in "off-the-grid" situations, disasters, and even day-to-day life. These ovens can be purchased or built as a DIY project, but they perform in the same way. By orienting reflective panels to redirect sunlight, this energy can be concentrated on a container. When the sun is strong, the best solar ovens can reach an internal temperature that exceeds 400°F. This is a steamy baking method, capable of creating slow-cooked meats and very moist baked goods. If you're expecting to bake a crispy loaf bread in this oven, you'll be disappointed. But if you're looking for a gooey pan of brownies, and you can wait two hours, this cooking method is perfect.

1 **(18.3-ounce) (530 g) box brownie mix**
Vegetable oil
Eggs
Nonstick cooking spray

1. In a large bowl combine the brownie mix, oil, and egg called for in the package directions, omitting the water. Stir until smooth.

2. Lightly spray an 8x8-inch (20x20-cm) baking pan with cooking spray (make sure the pan fits into the solar oven). Pour batter into prepared pan.

3. Place pan in the solar oven. Bake 2 hours, reorienting the oven with the sun every 15 to 20 minutes as it moves through the sky. Turn the oven away from the sun, open, and test with a wooden toothpick or nonpoisonous twig inserted near center; the brownies are done when it comes out clean. Continue baking for 20 minutes if not done. Let the brownies cool before cutting into 12 bars.

ADD FLAVOR AND TEXTURE TO THESE GOOEY DESSERT SQUARES WITH FAMILIAR ADDITIONS SUCH AS CHOCOLATE CHIPS AND/OR NUTS.

141 MAKE A CARDBOARD OVEN

Can't afford a factory-built solar oven? You can make your own, though the maximum burn temperature of a solar oven will only be half as hot as a commercial model. But the price is right. To make your own solar oven, you'll need foil, a cardboard box, a black cooking pot, a clear lid for the pot, tape, scissors to cut the box, a clear turkey cooking bag, and a clothespin. The heart of the operation is the pot, which absorbs the heat from sunlight reflected by the aluminum foil, while the pot sits inside the heat-resistant bag for a "greenhouse" effect. Cut the top from the box so it can be propped up, then tape aluminum foil on the interior of the entire cardboard box. Place a section of the turkey bag over the opening and tape it down. Place your black pot of food inside the box and keep it aimed toward the sun (move it every 30 minutes during the day).

142 COOK ON A RACK

When the storm of the century knocks out power and gas lines (or you've had to shut them off for safety), it may not seem like your faithful kitchen oven can help you cook anymore. But it can, and here are a couple of ways.

BUILD A BACKYARD GRILL After setting up a fire pit from rocks, bricks, cinder blocks, and other nonflammable materials, pull your racks out of your oven, and rest them over the top of your fire pit to turn the contraption into a functional grill. Light a fire underneath and commence cooking. The heavier gauge the wire, the more weight and heat your rack can handle. If it does start to sag, try flipping it over (to bend it the other way), decreasing the weight that it supports, or doubling up by adding a second rack on top.

SMOKE OUT YOUR OVEN If a grill isn't quite what you're looking for, you can even drag your poor old oven out into the yard entirely–with its racks still in place. Shovel some hot coals into the bottom of it, set your food on the racks above, and you'll be able to bake foods and even use it as an improvised meat smoker.

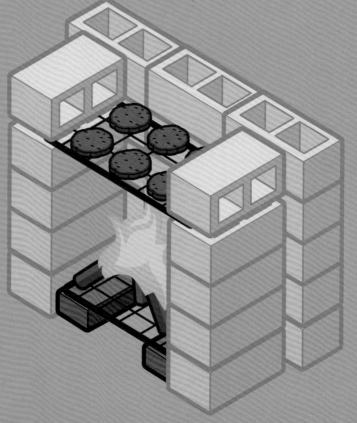

143 HACK A DISH

For those who are great fabricators, you can use your metalworking skills to turn an old satellite dish into your new parabolic cooker.

STEP 1 Decide how your dish will be set up and moved to follow the sun (just like the box cooker, you'll need to move it every 30 minutes or so to continue tracking the sun). You could build a tripod to support it, or mount the dish on a pole with a bracket.

STEP 2 Decide what you'll be cooking. If it's just meat, bolt a metal spike onto the arm so you can impale a big hunk. For more versatility, mount a flat piece of plate metal that you can set pots and kettles upon. Strip the electronics and wiring from the arm of the satellite dish.

STEP 3 Finish the project by covering the inside of the parabolic curve with mirrored tiles or strips of reflective metal, or glue on some aluminum foil. For the best effect, choose a dark-color cooking pot with all-metal construction. Plastic or rubberized handles can melt in the intense heat. Cover the dish when adding, stirring, or removing food so you don't get burned. A parabolic mirror can melt plastic and leave metal extremely hot on a bright day! Depending on the satellite dish size, your cooker may bake like an oven or slow-cook like a Crock Pot.

144 COOK LIKE A HOBO

Bottles and cans are abundant in the wild and after a disaster, and they can be collected and cleaned out to boil your water in a pinch. Glass bottles, beverage cans, and metal food cans will boil your water when you place them in the ashes next to a fire. Metal containers can also be placed on a grill over the fire. Don't try to suspend glass containers over the fire, as this intense heat can break the glass. You can even use snare wire or a piece of a coat hanger for a bail (handle) on a tin can cookpot. Use the tip of a knife or another sharp tool to pierce two holes near the opening of the can, on opposite sides. Cut a piece of wire and thread it through the holes. Bend each end so that the wire stays in place, and you're ready to hang your hobo cookpot over the fire. Be aware that some food cans will have a clear or white plastic lining, which is not something you want inside your cookpot. Place these cans in the fire for 10 to 20 minutes to burn it off, then sand or scrub the interior clean.

PAN-FRIED WORMS

SERVES 2

There are hundreds of different species of earthworm throughout the world. All are considered safe for human consumption, but they should be purged of the dirt that fills them before you try to eat them. An easy way to clean them out is to place them in a container of damp grass. After a few hours, the critters will be void of the dirt and sand they normally hold. Like all animal foods, worms should be cooked before you eat them, and I recommend frying as the method. Fried worms taste a little like worm jerky. The bad news: Worms are only about 1 calorie per gram (not counting any fat used for frying). The good news: Worms are high in protein, easy to identify, and abundant throughout much of the world.

Fresh green grass or salad greens
1½ tablespoons (12 g) cornmeal
10 large or 20 small live worms
3 ounces (90 ml) water
¼ pound (115 g) bacon
Fine salt

1. Place the grass or salad greens in a small container with a tight-fitting lid; add the cornmeal, worms, and just enough water to dampen the grass and cornmeal (you don't want a puddle in the bottom of the container). Leave them overnight in a cool location to allow the worms to purge the dirt, sand, and grit inside them and give themselves a cornmeal stuffing.

2. In a large skillet cook the bacon over medium-high heat until crisp. Transfer bacon to paper towels to drain. Leave grease in the skillet.

3. Add the worms to the skillet in a single layer and cook over medium heat until worms dry out, flatten, and become crisp, carefully stirring occasionally. Sprinkle with salt.

"THERE'S ALWAYS SOMETHING TO EAT, BUT IT MAY NOT BE ENOUGH OR WHAT YOU WANT TO EAT." T.M.

EVEN IN THE BLEAKEST CONDITIONS, THERE WILL BE THINGS YOU CAN CONSUME, BUT DEPENDING ON THE CONDITIONS, IT MAY NOT PROVIDE ENOUGH NUTRITION TO SUSTAIN YOU. IT ALSO MAY NOT BE YOUR DESIRED FOOD SOURCE. BE HAPPY WITH WHAT YOU HAVE, EVEN IF IT'S NOT MUCH—AND HANG IN THERE UNTIL THE CONDITIONS IMPROVE.

No fire or fuel is needed with a solar oven. Just place your food in the oven, close the door, align the box in the right orientation with the sun, and let the light do the rest.

STEP 1 Place a dark-color container of food inside the oven and close the door. Adjust the tilt of the oven, and orient it so that the reflectors are facing directly into the sun. Some units come with a "shadow" sighting attachment for perfect alignment.

STEP 2 Turn the oven once every 30 minutes to track the sun through the sky.

STEP 3 As the sun rises higher into the sky and then drops, raise or lower the zenith adjustment to match.

STEP 4 Allow the food to cook. It will usually take about four hours to bake bread. Tender roasts and baked apples will cook in about five hours. Savory soups and stews cook in about six hours.

146 HIJACK A CART

Whether you're preparing a feast to celebrate your survival after a major disaster, or you're just trying to eat up all your refrigerated food before it goes bad after a power outage, you'll want it to taste good. It's hard to "eat, drink, and be merry" in the face of destruction without something good to eat. Before those frozen steaks, sausages, and burgers thaw out and start to rot, create the grill to end all grills with an old metal shopping cart. You can burn firewood underneath the cart and use the bottom of the basket as the grill. You could also flip the cart on its side and burn a larger fire in the cart while using the side as a grill. Wipe down your improvised grill to clean it off similar to a standard barbecue grill grate. Keep some water nearby for fire safety, and use a shovel to move coals and burning chunks of wood in and out of the cart. Once it's ready, set food on the grill of the cart and start cooking. Try not to fuss with your food too much, especially the burgers. Don't flip them until they "release."

147 COOK IN YOUR CAR

A sunny day can turn a parked car into an oven, so why not use that heat? You don't have to do anything to turn your vehicle into a solar oven, and while it's usually not hot enough to cook meats or bread, it will heat up canned goods, MREs, and leftovers. Park your vehicle so that the windshield is facing south (in the northern hemisphere). Place your food on the dashboard and wait a few hours. If you place your lunch items out at breakfast, and set out your dinner foods at lunch, they'll have plenty of time to heat up. It doesn't have to be summer for this effect to work. With a 70°F (21°C) outdoor temperature, the interior can reach 104°F (40°C) in 30 minutes and 113°F (45°C) in one hour. And on a hot, sunny day, the interior can exceed 150°F (66°C).

148 COOK WITH YOUR CAR

If you've ever melted your favorite candy bar in your car, you know full well that a sunny day can turn a parked car into an oven. With a 70°F (21°C) outdoor temperature, the vehicle interior can reach 104°F (40°C) in 30 minutes and 113°F (45°C) in one hour. In warmer weather, the sun can heat the interior to more than 150°F (66°C) in less than two hours. This "slow cook" heat isn't usually hot enough to cook meats or bake bread, but can heat up canned goods, MREs, and leftovers. Park your vehicle so that the windshield is facing south (in the northern hemisphere). Place your food on the dashboard and wait a few hours. This can be a cool parlor trick, but the real magic show happens when you cook your food using the otherwise wasted heat of your vehicle's engine. Driving a vehicle (or even leaving it to idle) produces tremendous heat, some of which can be repurposed. You'll have best results with a car or truck engine, though creative survivors can also employ the engine on a boat, motorcycle, generator, or any other internal-combustion engine. This cooking technique will take some experimentation. It will also require some heavy-duty foil, bare wire, and pliers. Wrap your food in two separate layers of foil, and wire it in place somewhere in the engine compartment near the engine block. For foods that you'd like to sear, being near the exhaust manifold will provide higher heat. Being farther away from this component will keep your food in a cooler zone. Again, this will require some (or a lot of) experimentation on your part. Given all the different makes and models of vehicles on the planet (and all the different driving conditions), you'll just have to see what works for your car and the conditions.

CAR-NE ASADA

SERVES 4-6

Many English speakers are familiar with the Spanish word *carne*, which means meat. The word *asada* is a little less familiar, and it can be roughly translated to "roast" (though the dish we are about to prepare is frequently grilled, rather than roasted). If we put these words together, we get carne asada—a marinated beef steak that is loaded with authentic Mexican flavor. While this wonderful dish is steeped in both tradition and marinade, we can easily adapt it for a nontraditional cooking technique. Let's build a foil-packet recipe with Latin flair, and cook under the hood of a running vehicle. It's "car"ne asada!

1 cup (16 g) chopped fresh cilantro leaves and tender stems

½ cup (120 ml) orange juice

¼ cup (60 ml) olive oil

Juice of 3 limes

2 tablespoons (30 ml) white wine vinegar

4 cloves garlic, crushed

1 tablespoon (5 g) freshly grated ginger

1 teaspoon (5 g) salt

¼ teaspoon (0.5 g) freshly ground black pepper

1 jalapeño, finely chopped

2 pounds (900 g) flank steak or other red meat

1. In a gallon-size resealable plastic bag combine all of the ingredients except for the meat. Shake briefly to combine. Add the meat and turn to coat. Marinate in the refrigerator for at least 3 hours or up to overnight. Drain meat, leaving some marinade on the meat; discard remaining marinade.

2. Wrap the meat in two layers of aluminum foil; fold into a packet. Wire the packet under the hood of a vehicle. Drive 10 to 20 minutes (10 minutes in hot weather, 20 minutes in colder weather). Carefully turn the packet over and secure. Drive until a thermometer inserted in the thickest portion reads 145°F (63°C) for medium-rare or 160°F (71°C) for medium, 5 to 10 minutes (depending upon hot/cold weather).

3. Remove packet from the engine. Let the packet stand for 5 minutes. Remove meat from the packet and slice against the grain.

THIS COOKING TECHNIQUE IS BEST SUITED FOR WARM WEATHER. DRIVING IN EXTREME COLD WILL CAUSE FRIGID AIR TO MOVE THROUGH THE ENGINE COMPARTMENT AND MAY PREVENT SAFE COOKING TEMPERATURES FROM BEING REACHED.

149 FEED THE CRITTERS

You ran out of dry kibble during a calamity? Survival cooking in modern society doesn't just mean having to take care of yourself and your human family. In many parts of the world, people also have animal-family members, cat or dog "children," or other small fuzzy friends (to say nothing of reptiles, birds, fish, bugs, etc.), and in a survival scenario they also need to eat. But your survival situation doesn't need to become more complicated with starving or inadvertently poisoned pets. Once you run out of kibble for your cat, or your 50-pound bag of dog food is empty, you might not be able to get more; short of letting them go feral, you need to feed your companions. Long before the commercial availability of mass-produced dog food, people fed their dogs many of the same foods that they were eating. And just as we crave good taste and variety, so do our pets. That's why they beg for table scraps! But which human foods can you safely give

your dog? Cooked meats and cooked eggs are great sources of fat and protein for poochie. Many fresh or frozen vegetables can be finely chopped and added to their food for fiber, vitamins, and minerals. Just avoid onions, garlic, and avocados. They don't need sweets either, so skip the grapes, raisins, and of course chocolate. These and a few other people foods are toxic to dogs. You'll also want to skip the canned veggies and fruits. These are often high in sugar and sodium, and their mushy texture can cause stomach upset in dogs and cats. Just do your best to mimic the natural diet of the species. Your pet rat, for example, is an omnivore, happy to nibble on almost any food source. Reptiles will need much more specialized foods, depending on their regular diet (some being nearly vegetarian, while others eat mostly animal-based food). Plan ahead for your pets just as much as you will plan for your human companions.

150 DO THE DISHES

Another important aspect of both cooking and survival is cleaning up! After your post-disaster dinner, you're still going to have dishes to do (especially when the paper plates and plastic forks are all gone!). Dirty dishes and cooking containers aren't just unpleasant. They can pose a serious health risk. If bacteria and other pathogens are allowed to proliferate on food-smeared plates, bowls, cutlery, and cookware, they can contaminate the cooked food that touches them. This can cause mild problems, like digestive upset. It can also cause major problems, ones that could potentially be fatal in austere conditions. All it takes is a few of the wrong organisms to cause dysentery or bacterial meningitis during a survival situation. So what's the cure? Do your dishes, folks! Whether you're just practicing your self-reliance skills to get ready for a television survival show or you're embroiled in a real disaster, potable running water may be at a minimum. Consider using grass, leaves, pine needles, or crumpled-up scrap paper to wipe away food residue that can't be scraped off with your utensils. Then scrub the dish surface with a bleach-and-water solution on a rag (one part bleach and nine parts water). Allow the dishes to dry in direct sunlight, as the UV radiation can kill dangerous organisms. And for all metal cookware and dishes, you can minimize your water consumption while still getting the maximum cleanliness by heating the "clean" dishes by a fire to disinfect them.

151 SKIP THE SOAP

After teaching a long survival class during cold weather, the simple act of washing my filthy hands with soap and unlimited warm water is one of my favorite things in the world. The soap-and-water combo is something we often take for granted, until we've had to live without it. But it is possible to get by without these wonderful resources. You even want to avoid using soap for certain surfaces. Take cast-iron cookware, for example. It's a terrible idea to soak a food-caked cast-iron pot in soapy water. This volatile combination will begin to strip away the "seasoning" on the iron's surface. It can take months or even years to build up a nonstick oil-and-carbon seasoning layer on cast iron, and typical washing practices tend to erode it. Instead of getting after the pot with a soapy sponge, heat the pot again with your heat source and wipe it clean with a washable cloth and a little water. You could also scrub it very gently while it's warm, with an oil-soaked cloth. I prefer grapeseed oil, as it tends to dry in the air (rather than becoming a sticky mess). You could also try a bit of salt and a crumpled ball of aluminum foil as a scrubbing tool for cast iron and other cookware.

CREAMY OYSTER STEW

SERVES 4

Growing up, oyster stew was a familiar dish here in the Mid-Atlantic. We wouldn't have it often. In fact, Mom would usually only make a small pot of it for Dad around New Year's Day (and that was it for the year). This was enough to lodge the scent and memory deep in my mind. The simple stew she would create was little more than oysters, milk and butter, but the briny aroma would fill the kitchen, and I do believe it primed me to be a seafood lover as an adult. Oysters haven't always been a food for special occasions. Centuries ago they were viewed as an undesirable food only eaten to stave off starvation. When the Spanish first came to the East Coast, only the most desperate diners would eat these saline bottom-feeders. Today, however, oysters are served raw at high-end establishments, and they are the basis of soups and stews that make clam chowder look like, well, clam chowder.

5 tablespoons (75 g) unsalted butter

2 tablespoons (16 g) all-purpose flour

1 small onion, finely chopped

1 stalk celery, finely chopped (a few leaves reserved, if available)

1 medium carrot, finely chopped

¾ cup (180 ml) water

1 (12-ounce) (355-ml) can evaporated milk

3 (8-ounce) (120-ml) cans whole oysters in water, liquid reserved

1 teaspoon (3 g) garlic powder

½ teaspoon (1 g) dried thyme

½ teaspoon (1 g) black pepper

¼ to ½ teaspoon (0.5 to 1 g) crushed red pepper

¼ teaspoon (1 g) salt, plus more to taste

Chopped fresh parsley, for garnishing

Oyster crackers or crusty bread, for serving

1. In a large saucepan melt the butter over medium heat. Slowly whisk flour into the melted butter until well combined; cook for 2 minutes, stirring constantly. Add onion, celery, and carrot; cook, stirring frequently, for 4 minutes. Slowly stir in the water, evaporated milk, and oyster liquid. Reduce the heat to low, and simmer for 5 minutes.

2. Add whole oysters, garlic powder, thyme, black pepper, crushed red pepper, and salt to the liquid. Increase the heat to medium-high and bring to almost boiling (but do not boil or the soup will curdle). Reduce the heat and simmer until edges of the oysters begin to curl, about 5 minutes.

3. Finely chop reserved celery leaves, if using. Sprinkle servings of soup with celery leaves and/or chopped parsley. Serve with crackers or crusty bread.

OYSTERS AREN'T THE ONLY OPTION FOR THIS RICH STEW. USE ANY OTHER SEAFOOD RESOURCE IF YOU LACK THE STAR INGREDIENT.

152 BREW YOUR OWN ALCOHOL

Home brewing is much easier than you think, and once you stock up on the right yeast, the rest of the supplies are probably close at hand. The resulting brew could be worth a lot in tough times–homespun alcohol can disinfect, anesthetize, and lubricate bartering deals, to name just a few of its many uses.

To put it briefly, you're going to add yeast to a sugar-water solution, which is kept at room temperature. The yeast is going to eat the sugar, producing carbon dioxide and alcohol. This is the process of fermentation, which will last about a month. During this time, a special cap will let the CO_2 bubble out but keep oxygen from entering the brewing jug. Sounds simple, right? It is.

COLLECT YOUR SUPPLIES You'll need a 1-gallon (4-l) glass jug, yeast, a sugar source (honey, malt, table sugar, molasses), clean water, and a wine lock cap for the jug. One other item of note is a sanitizer; a quick fix is cheap vodka. The wine lock is the only part that may need to be improvised (if you don't pick one up when you buy your yeast). It can be a vinyl hose that fits into or over the mouth of the jug. Another popular option is a balloon that has been pierced by a needle. When the balloon fills with CO_2, the needle hole opens and relieves the pressure like a valve.

BE SWEET If you intend to brew beer that tastes like beer, you'll need malt. This can be found in a can with hops already added or as a powdered extract. For old-school brewing, you could sprout some grains like wheat or barley, then toast and grind them. Simmer the ground grain in water for an hour, and filter out the malt-rich water, which then boils with the hops for another hour. If you're making wine, you can use a mix of fruit and table sugar. For mead, all you need is honey and water (plus wine yeast). Almost any sugar will ferment.

GET CARBONATED To make your beer bubble or your champagne fizz, you will need to carbonate it after fermentation. This can be done by adding more sugar to the brew and sealing it in a pressure-safe vessel. The dormant yeast will wake up to produce a little more CO_2, carbonating the beverage. Add an ounce of table sugar or corn sugar to each gallon of brew, and seal it in bottles. Clean soda bottles and self-capping ones will work fine. Let it sit for one week, then chill and enjoy.

153 LOCK IT DOWN

Airlocks are a necessary cap on any fermentation jug or vessel. Store bought versions commonly feature an S-shaped water trap, just like you have under your sink. The CO_2-rich air can bubble out through the water in the lock, but the oxygen-rich air can't get back inside (to sour your brew). I also like to use a vinyl tube going into a glass of water for an air lock when brewing foamy beer. The foam would push the water out of a normal airlock, but dissolves into the glass of water instead. You can even use a balloon with a pinhole pierced into it for an air lock. Stretch the mouth of the balloon over the jug opening and secure it with a few rubber bands. As the CO_2 builds inside the balloon, it swells up. Once enough pressure is achieved, the pinhole will allow some of it to hiss out. Once the pressure drops again, the hole closes. Again, just make sure you have secured the balloon so it cannot pop off the top, exposing and spoiling your fermenting brew.

CRAFT AN AMBER ALE

YOU'LL NEED

- **1   pound (450 g) dried amber malt extract**
- **¼   ounce (7 g) Cascade hops**
- **1   package ale yeast**
- **1   ounce (28 g) sugar to carbonate the ale**
- **Bottles to handle the pressure of carbonation**

STEP 1 In a big stainless-steel or enamel pot, boil 1 gallon (4 l) of water with the malt extract and the Cascade hops for 60 minutes. (Watch that it doesn't boil over!)

STEP 2 Cool and strain the brew into a clean jug. Let it cool to room temperature, as it needs to be below 80°F (27°C) before adding the yeast.

STEP 3 Add the dried yeast to the brew and shake it up. Use ale yeast to brew at room temperature. Lager yeast will require holding the temp at 50°–55°F (10°–13°C) for an extended two-month fermentation.

STEP 4 Add the sanitized fermentation lock to the vessel. Watch carefully for a few days. If bubbling (fermentation) doesn't occur in 12 to 24 hours, your yeast was dead, or the too-hot heat killed it. Add more yeast to save the batch.

STEP 5 Set the jug in a sink for a few days, as the malt-and-hops combo will foam over. After a week, clean the air lock and replace it. Three weeks later, the sediment should be thick at the bottom, the bubbling should have stopped, and the ale should be clearing.

STEP 6 Pour the flat beer into a clean container, leaving the sediment in the jug. Add 1 ounce of sugar per gallon of beer and mix. Funnel into sanitized bottles and cap them. You'll need about 10 bottles (12-ounce size) and caps for 1 gallon of ale. Keep the beer at room temperature for one week to carbonate, then chill for one more week and enjoy.

STIR-FRY A SCAVENGER

SERVES 6

Here's the bad news first: Raccoons are some of the most disease-infested wild game animals in North America. They often carry the rabies virus, though they may be asymptomatic. They also harbor an intestinal roundworm that is communicable to humans. Here's the good news, though: Their diverse diet makes their meat one of the most nutrient-rich protein sources in the animal kingdom (high in many vitamins and minerals). When raccoons eat a clean diet in the wild (not too much garbage), they also have a pleasant flavor (similar to dark-meat chicken, though greasier). Wear disposable gloves, process carefully, and cook until well done, and your raccoon stir-fry will be the talk of your survival camp.

FOR THE RACCOON:

1	raccoon, skinned, cleaned, fat removed, and trimmed of musk glands
¼	cup (60 ml) white vinegar
4	cloves garlic
2	tablespoons (30 g) salt
2	tablespoons (20 g) peppercorns

FOR THE STIR-FRY:

2	tablespoons (30 ml) vegetable oil
1	medium yellow onion, chopped
2	cups (200 g) white mushrooms, halved
2	cups (130 g) small cauliflower florets
1	large zucchini, cut into ¼-inch (6 mm) pieces
2	carrots, cut into matchsticks
¼	cup (60 ml) light soy sauce
1	tablespoon (15 ml) sesame oil
1	teaspoon (2 g) black pepper
¼	cup (35 g) chopped toasted cashews
4	scallions, cut on the diagonal
	Hot cooked rice, for serving

1. For the raccoon: In a large stockpot add the raccoon and water to cover. Add the vinegar, garlic, salt, and peppercorns. Bring the water to boiling over high heat. Gently boil, covered, for 1 hour or until meat is tender. Drain raccoon and cut into ¾-inch (18-mm) pieces.

2. For stir-fry: In an extra-large skillet cook onion, mushrooms, cauliflower, zucchini, and carrots in hot oil over medium-high heat, stirring constantly, for 3 minutes. Add raccoon meat and stir to combine. Cook until vegetables are tender-crisp, 3 to 4 minutes.

3. Add soy sauce, sesame oil, and black pepper; stir to combine. Top servings with cashews and scallions. Serve stir-fry over rice.

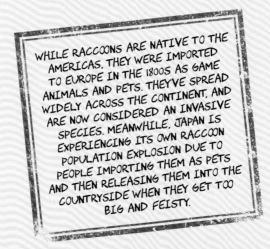

WHILE RACCOONS ARE NATIVE TO THE AMERICAS, THEY WERE IMPORTED TO EUROPE IN THE 1800S AS GAME ANIMALS AND PETS. THEY'VE SPREAD WIDELY ACROSS THE CONTINENT, AND ARE NOW CONSIDERED AN INVASIVE SPECIES. MEANWHILE, JAPAN IS EXPERIENCING ITS OWN RACCOON POPULATION EXPLOSION DUE TO PEOPLE IMPORTING THEM AS PETS AND THEN RELEASING THEM INTO THE COUNTRYSIDE WHEN THEY GET TOO BIG AND FEISTY.

155 STEP IT UP

It's fun (and tasty) to make your own hard cider from apples and other fruits. You'll just need to buy or borrow a cider press, or get creative and make one.

STEP 1 Squeeze the chopped and mashed fruit in the press to extract the sugar-rich juice; you can feed the solids to your livestock if you have any. Pour your juice into a large enamel or stainless-steel pot.

STEP 2 Heat the juice to boiling for 30 minutes to kill any stray wild yeast or bacteria, then let it cool to room temperature.

STEP 3 Add a packet of cider yeast or wine yeast to the cool juice, and stir with a sanitized spoon. Pour the juice into a large sanitized glass jug. Add a water-filled air lock on top.

STEP 4 Let it bubble for 45 days, then pour the cider off the top (leaving the sediment) and enjoy the fruits of your labor: a tasty adult beverage you made for yourself!

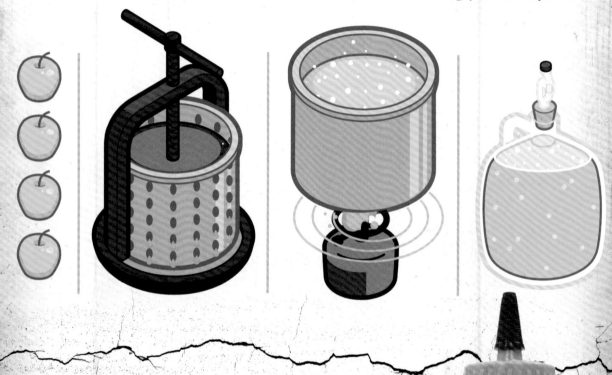

156 BREW MEAD

YOU'LL NEED

2½ pounds (1 kg) honey
1 gallon (4 l) water
1 package champagne yeast

In a large stainless-steel or enamel pot, bring the honey and water to a boil. Boil for 10 minutes, skimming off any foam that forms on top (you can eat this; it's tasty). Cool the liquid to room temperature, then add the Champagne yeast. Use a sanitized funnel to pour the brew into a sanitized glass or food-grade plastic fermentation vessel, and attach the wine lock. Let it ferment for six weeks (honey is slow).

After it has fermented and cleared, drain the mead into a sanitized jug, and cork or cap it securely. Age for a few months in a cool, dark place, then enjoy the king's nectar.

157 BE FRUGAL

"Waste not, want not"—this little saying from the 1700s essentially means that if you do not waste anything, you will always have enough. Being frugal can be tricky, but there are some easy ways to save money, time, and resources when you brew. For example, you could sprout your own barley and other grains to create homemade malt. This building block for beer is cheap, and once you've pulled the sugar out for brewing, you can feed the leftover grain to your livestock. And let's say you didn't have enough fruit or berry juice to do an all-juice batch of wine. Don't worry; you can use table sugar to make your wine stronger. Mix 2 pounds (1 kg) each of sugar and fruit juice with enough water to make 1 gallon (4 l) of wine. But what if you run out of yeast packets? Most stores don't carry wine and beer yeast, just bread yeast (which doesn't produce as much alcohol). But fruit skins carry yeast, and we can just toss a few chalky-looking raw fruits into the cooled-down batch of boiled brew to provide some wild yeast. It's a gamble to the risk the flavor this way, as certain strains can produce some strange flavors; the wrong one can leave your brew tasting like Band-Aids. On the other hand, your concoction might taste like butterscotch with the right strain.

MAKE YOUR OWN FUEL

Whether serving as a small light source or powering an improvised camping stove, those cans of Sterno are a great resource. With a few household ingredients, you can make your own by creating a substance that binds with alcohol to make a gel.

YOU'LL NEED

Antacid tablets with a minimum of 1,000 mg calcium carbonate each

White vinegar

Alcohol of at least 95% (ethanol, grain alcohol, or isopropyl rubbing alcohol)

STEP 1 Crush your antacid tablets into fine powder. (You can substitute crushed eggshells, powdered gardener's lime, or calcium supplements.)

STEP 2 Add vinegar to the powder, about 2 teaspoons (10 ml) per tablet, and stir until the powder dissolves and the fizzing stops. Allow it to dry overnight and thicken into a slurry; its volume will shrink by half.

STEP 3 Measure out an amount of alcohol about twice the volume of the slurry, and stir in slowly and thoroughly, a bit at a time. The mixture will thicken into a jelly.

STEP 4 Collect into a container, and seal it airtight to avoid any alcohol evaporation. When needed, you can open the container and light the material (after placing into a fireproof vessel, if needed).

WILD TEAS

SERVES 1

A cup of tea may not seem like much sustenance, but the right tea can provide great flavor and some significant nutrition. And there's no better way to get medicinal plant compounds into your body than drinking a warm mug of wild medicine tea. The hot water used to make the tea can draw out the plant compounds better than cold water. These teas can even replace the water lost by ailments that cause diarrhea, profuse sweating, and vomiting. Yes, tea can be enjoyed for the taste and used to maintain good health, but there seems to be some confusion about tea making (at least in the foraging and survival realms). Many people complain about their wild tea tasting bad. After a few quick questions, I usually figure out that it was the process (not the materials) that tripped them up. Follow these brewing guidelines, and you'll produce outstanding teas.

Teas are made through a process called infusion. This means that the plant material soaks in hot water, like a scalding hot bath. Never boil your tea! If you do, you're making a decoction, which is generally not for drinking. Decoctions are typically used as a topical remedy, outside the body.

Don't ignore water quality and safety. If you're making tea out of water from a stream or other wild source, boil it for 10 minutes, then remove it from the heat before you add the plants. This way, you've disinfected the water, but you've not boiled your tea materials.

Keep it covered! Any kind of lid on the tea vessel will help to keep the light, volatile oils in your brew. These oils are responsible for a good portion of your tea's flavor. Open tea pots contribute to lost flavor.

Look at Your Choices

Plenty of commercial herbal teas are used to help with health complaints. But which wild tea is right for your ailments? Look at this list, and what's growing around you, to find the right plant for your needs.

Peppermint (*Mentha piperita*): This tea is excellent at soothing an upset stomach. Add 1 tablespoon (0.5 g) dried leaf or 2 tablespoons (1 g) fresh leaf to 1 cup (240 ml) hot water; cover and steep for 10 to 15 minutes. It also helps with hangovers. Warning: Pregnant or nursing women; anyone with gastroesophageal reflux disease (GERD); or anyone with liver disease should avoid ingesting strong peppermint teas or products.

American ginseng (*Panax quinquifolius*): Teas from different species of ginseng are used in many countries as a tonic and energy booster. Two teaspoons dried ginseng root steeped in 1 cup (240 ml) hot water for 30 minutes will provide you with a tea that revitalizes and invigorates. It's even touted as an aphrodisiac, though your results may vary.

Pine needle (*Pinus spp.*): Stave off scurvy with this survival classic. Pine needle tea is loaded with vitamin C. Two tablespoons (4 g) chopped fresh pine needles added to 1 cup (240 ml) hot water will give you a tea in 15 minutes and has five times the USDA daily allowance of vitamin C. Warning: Pregnant women, or women who may be pregnant, should not drink pine needle tea as it may be abortive.

BEER

1 BOIL WATER One man's trash ... right? Just a single cast-off beer can is capable of becoming a life saver, if the can is used to boil raw water to make it safe for human consumption. The trick with boiling in cans is to set the water-filled can next to the fire in the ashes. Do not place the can in the center of the fire, as the metal will break down quicker. In 10 or 15 minutes, the water will start to boil. Then just boil for 10 additional minutes to be on the safe side. Let the water cool, and have yourself a pathogen-free drink.

2 SKIN CLEANSING Aside from cooking with beer (which adds flavor and moisture), beer can be used to irrigate wounds and wash skin. It's even been used as the first bath water for babies, in a few cultures around the world.

3 REFLECTIVE SIGNAL If your beer can isn't shiny on the outside, cut the thing in half to expose the metallic interior. It's not going to be as shiny as a signal mirror, but it still can reflect light as a form of signaling for help. It can also be hung up in a prominent place, to twist in the wind, as an "automated" distress signal.

4 CANDLE LANTERN A short candle and a creatively carved-up can will give you a surprising amount of light in your survival camp. Just cut the side out of the can, add a handful of sand, stick a candle chunk inside the lantern, and light it. Hang your lantern from the pull tab on a nearby twig, or hang it from a piece of wire.

5 FISH HOOK Break off the can's pull tab, and cut out a section of tab so that it looks like a fish hook. Sharpen the hook tip to a point, attach it to your line, and bait it appropriately. Instead of trying to set the hook in the fish's mouth when he bites, give some line and let the fish swallow the hook. The pull-tab hook will hang up on the soft stomach or esophagus a lot better than it would pierce the fish's jaw. Be advised that this is not a catch and release method, as you'll probably pull out the fish's guts while retrieving the hook.

6 SURVIVAL STOVE Cut a can in half, add a few ounces of high-test alcohol to the bottom half, and you've got yourself a dollar-friendly camping stove. No, it won't preform like a Jet boil, but the price is right. You can also prowl the internet for plans to build a can stove with little jets around the top lip, which will increase the stove's efficiency.

7 PROJECTILE POINT More dangerous than a wooden point, any sharp projectile point can add damage to an arrow or spear impact. You could even fashion the harpoon tip to be detachable, and run a line off of it. Cut the can into different size and shape pieces, and fold the pieces into cones and flat triangles to assist in small-game hunting during survival situations. But obviously, a beer can does not a broad head make. Stick to the little critters on this one.

8 BEER AS BAIT Slugs, snails, and many other bugs just can't seem to resist beer. Pour out a little pan of brew, or leave a few ounces in the bottom of the can to collect bugs for fish bait, trap bait, a desperate man's stew, or pest control in your survival garden.

9 SAFE HYDRATION Beer has been used for thousands of years as a pathogen-free beverage.

10 STORED CALORIES Beer has long been a way to store food calories that kept the critters out. You could have a barrel of wheat or barley in your little shack, which you could never keep the rats and bugs out of. Or you could have a barrel of beer that still had much of the same calorie value, and wouldn't even be tainted if a rat or bug ended up bobbing around in there.

RODENT BBQ SANDWICH

SERVES 4 TO 6

As rodents go, most are mild-flavored and pleasant enough to eat in a wide variety of ways. Sadly, this just isn't the case for groundhog. Also known as the whistle pig, land beaver, and most commonly—woodchuck, these animals possess many small scent glands that can impart gamey flavors into the cooked meat. These musky glands can be seen in the "armpits," down its back, and near the tail end. These pungent pea-sized nodules should all be removed during gutting and skinning as quickly as possible. For even better results, soak your cleaned woodchuck in salted water in a refrigerator overnight. And just in case you missed a gland or two, it's very helpful to be sitting on a stockpile of your favorite spicy BBQ sauce. The following recipe is designed for a Dutch oven for campfire cooking, but it can also be adapted to a slow cooker (see Note).

1	medium yellow onion, diced
2	tablespoons (30 g) butter
4	cloves garlic, minced
1	teaspoon dried thyme (1 g) or 2 teaspoons (2 g) minced fresh thyme
1	teaspoon (2 g) fennel seeds
1	teaspoon (5 g) salt
1	teaspoon (2 g) freshly ground black pepper
2	groundhogs, cleaned and quartered
1	cup (240 ml) chicken stock or broth
1	recipe Classic BBQ Sauce or 1 bottle barbecue sauce

1. In a Dutch oven cook the onion in butter over a medium fire until tender. Add the garlic, thyme, fennel, salt, and black pepper.

2. Place the groundhog meat in the Dutch oven; add the stock. Place the Dutch oven over a bed of hot coals that are maintained (by adding more coals periodically) and cook until the meat is falling off the bone, 2 to 3 hours.

3. Generously slather the meat with barbecue sauce before serving on buns.

Classic BBQ Sauce: In a medium saucepan stir together 1 (15-ounce) (443-ml) can tomato sauce, one (6-ounce) (177-ml) can tomato paste, ⅓ cup (80 ml) cider vinegar, ¼ cup (60 ml) maple syrup, ¼ cup (60 ml) molasses, 2 tablespoons (30 ml) Worcestershire sauce, 2 teaspoons (4 g) paprika, 1 teaspoon (2 g) dry mustard, 1 teaspoon (3 g) garlic powder, ½ teaspoon (1 g) onion powder, ½ teaspoon (1 g) black pepper, and ¼ teaspoon (1 g) salt. Bring to a simmer over medium-high heat. Reduce heat to medium-low and simmer, partially covered and stirring occasionally, until the sauce thickens, about 10 to 15 minutes. Use immediately, or let cool and store in an airtight container in the refrigerator for up to 1 week.

Note: You can also cook the onion in a skillet; add the garlic, thyme, fennel, salt, and black pepper. Transfer onion mixture to a slow cooker. Add groundhogs; cover and cook on high for 3 hours or low for 6 hours. Generously slather the meat with barbecue sauce before serving.

THE GROUNDHOG THRIVES IN THE NORTHERN UNITED STATES AS WELL AS CANADA AND ALASKA. IT IS RELATED TO EUROPEAN AND ASIAN MARMOTS, WHICH HAVE BEEN EATEN FOR CENTURIES BY INDIGENOUS PEOPLES. BE SURE TO COOK THE MEAT THOROUGHLY; PEOPLE IN MONGOLIA AND SIBERIA HAVE GOTTEN THE PLAGUE FROM EATING RAW MARMOT FLESH.